My Bipolar Life

Jane
by
joanne Adams

My Bipolar Life

Jane S

Bent Twig Books • Tyrone, Pennsylvania

My Bipolar Life

Bent Twig Books
A division of Perkunas Press
2635 Baughman Cemetery Road
Tyrone, Pennsylvania 16686
USA

http://bent-twig-books.com/

Author contact: https://janesabc.wordpress.com/

Trade Paperback
ISBN-13: 978-1-62962-054-1
ISBN-10: 1-62962-054-8

Library of Congress Control Number: 2017961891

ALSO BY JANE S.

Q&A: Alcoholism & Sobriety

See https://janesabc.wordpress.com/ for more information.

FOR MY PARENTS
KATHRYN AND EDWARD S.

Keep yourself like an empty vessel for God to fill. Keep pouring out yourself to help others so that God can keep filling you up with His spirit.... To be clear, a lake must have an inflow and an outflow.—*Twenty-Four Hours a Day*, Nov. 2nd.

Every man according as he purposeth in his heart, so let him give, not grudgingly nor of necessity, for God loveth a cheerful giver—*II Corinthians* 9:7

CONTENTS

A WORD FROM THE AUTHOR

If you suffer from bipolar disorder (manic depression), or if someone you love suffers, my story may help save your life—or theirs. It wasn't just personal stories alone that helped me—except by letting me know there were others in the same fix I was in. But personal stories with explanations and parallels drawn—they helped me understand.

It's been said that 60 percent of those with bipolar disorder may be alcoholic, and 60 percent of alcoholics may be bipolar. I'm one of the many "bipolars" with alcohol problems, and in Alcoholics Anonymous we try to tell our stories so they'll help other alcoholics. I've tried to tell my story here so there are clues to successfully beating back the manic depression (and alcoholism is part of my story: that's here too.) I hope to help everyone who is bipolar as much as I can, but I'm alcoholic *and* bipolar: there may be extra life-saving help here for those who are both.

When I stopped drinking, and learned to keep stopped, through Alcoholics Anonymous, I thought my problems were over. They weren't. A little over a year and a half later, I was hospitalized, as is told in "My Story," which leads off this book, after this brief author's word.

When I was diagnosed as a manic-depressive, I had three questions I think every newly-diagnosed manic depressive has—I mean, besides the usual "Why does this have to happen to <u>me</u>?" They were (1) "What is manic depression [bipolar disorder]?" and (2) "What can I do about it—how is it treated?" and (3) "How can I live

1

my life with this horrible condition?" (Some of my friends may not have asked this third question out loud, but they decided the answer was that they couldn't. They answered the question with suicide. If you have the disease, you'll know why.). As a manic depressive who was and is also alcoholic, I also wanted to know (4) "Is there a link between my two diseases?" I'll tell my story, and then I'll try to answer these questions in notes.

MY STORY

It isn't very exciting, but I'll begin at the beginning—except I'll put in three vignettes from years later.

The first vignette—maybe "vision" would be a better word—is most obviously from the alcoholism part of my story, though I know now it's from both. It was the night I stopped drinking, in October 1970. For almost the first night in years, I didn't have a nightmare—I had what I now think of as my white dream (and I'm afraid I'm having to tell the story in the same words I use later on—it's hard enough to find one set of words). In the dream there was a large window with no curtains and glistering white sunlight poured in that window almost as white as diamonds. I had never had a dream like that before (or since)—what was it like? Even the words I have found don't seem to describe what happened very well. I saw the light, though I can't really describe its appearance (even "white" isn't quite right), and as soon as I saw it, it was like the design of things was opened to me. I sat there, all confused, and then my whole self that had been angry and "down" was suddenly "up"—like a switch from drowning to swimming.

In the second vignette, maybe twenty months later, I'm in a padded side-room in the mental hospital and I'm convinced my head is detached and bouncing around the room. (I think now it was from the sounds of a volley-ball game outside, but back then it was my head and it was bouncing off the walls.) This is obviously part of the "bipolar" part of my story.

3

The third vignette is in the same part of the bipolar story. I'm in the same (mental) hospital (my last one), beginning the lithium treatment (which had just recently been re-approved in the United States). This is only a short time after the bouncing volleyball-head. After a few days in solitary confinement I was allowed to wear real clothes and my meals were upstairs. Eventually I was allowed down the huge staircase to the dining room and after all I'd been through the dining room was like a palace and I could eat anything I wanted and even have seconds.

But when they began to introduce the lithium carbonate, I did not do well. I had tremendous tremors and it was nothing for me to take a spoonful of cereal and the tremor would be so great the cereal wound up thrown across the room. I can still see that and the table I was sitting at. Then one day the nurse came up to me with a little plate of crackers covered with peanut butter. There were about half a dozen crackers on the plate—no, maybe four or five. I asked what they were for and I was told just to eat the crackers: the doctor had ordered them. After a week or two my tremors were gone and with just a few minor exceptions they have not returned. That was something more than forty years ago.

So there are the parts of the "trailer" for my story. A wonderful vision, then my head as a bouncing volley-ball, and then fooling my system by putting Lithium in peanut-butter on crackers. Back to my story.

BEGINNING: CHILDHOOD/YOUTH TO DADDY'S DEATH

I was born June 26 1941, on just about the hottest day in years, in Chestnut Hill, Philadelphia, to two intelligent loving parents. Two years later my brother was born (on a colder day, in October) and he had the same conditions I have—manic depression and alcoholism. But he developed differently.

I seemed to be able to get along pretty well with my dad but the situation with my mother was crazy. I guess she had no idea how to handle me so she beat me. I got more spankings—lickings—beatings than you could shake a stick at. I had bruises, black and blue marks everywhere and I was terribly ashamed and I never told a living soul. I was afraid to tell my father for fear he would be angry with my mother so I just lived it out. My brother was very much like me but he never got a spanking. Maybe because he was asthmatic (and two years younger).

I think I started yelling and screaming when I was born in the Chestnut Hill hospital—as I say, it was the hottest time of the hottest year then on record, and my grandfather had my mother and me to stay at the house on the Widener Estate, where he lived as the Superintendent of the Estate: it was cooler there with the stone house and the trees around the house. (This house comes back into the story when I didn't even recognize it years later.) And my grandfather taught my mother how to stop my crying by holding me up with my stomach on the palm of his hand and his arm raised. It worked.

The house where I spent my early days, from age four to age thirteen, was also large. It was a couple of hundred years old and had two fireplaces and seven bedrooms. I shared this house with my mother and father, my baby brother, my cousin Stephanie when she stayed with us, and our housekeeper Iva.

I started very early with temper tantrums (which I was famous for in our family) and gave my mother a lot of trouble. I picked on my brother Teddy all the time, and my cousin Stephanie when she was there. The main reason I picked on Stevie was that she had cascades of curling hair and I had none (and seventy years later I still don't have any). When I started to school I had trouble getting along with everyone, teachers and students, though I got good grades and played sports.

It was when I was almost thirteen that my father died suddenly of a heart attack and I was left with my mother and brother. I went to work in my father's greenhouses and I missed school: there wasn't much normal in my life at thirteen.

Up to that time there hadn't been other people in my life besides family (but I had twenty first-cousins): instead of friends I had dolls. And a doll crib and a doll coach. And a large bedroom with lots of books. And, of course, dogs—and there were the horses. But no people friends. I worried about what was wrong with me and as a matter of fact I still do, though now I have a diagnosis, a condition called manic depression.

Shortly after my father died, my brother was sent to the Milton Hershey School and I was left with my mother. (There wasn't anyone else to take care of the greenhouses.) In seventh grade in the junior high school, before I quit to work in the greenhouses, I spoke when I should not have spoken to Mr. S, the art teacher, and he slapped me. I was absolutely shocked. I didn't say anything but I was terrified. This was right after my dad died and before I started work at the greenhouses. I don't think I went back to school. I was humiliated and I didn't even tell my mother. I must have really tried his patience.

I did talk out of turn in every class I was in—I even "spoke out" in one of Mr. Risser's classes at the Prospectville School (he was our Principal). When I did that (this was before my dad died), Mr. Risser came over toward me and I ran out of the room and into the girls' room. That was the day he called my father. My father told Mr. Risser, "Tell her to go home immediately." I did and he came home and he spanked me, which was very rare.

There were two times my father spanked me—that time and the time I came home from seventh grade and I spoke of the African-American boy in my class using the n-word, because that's the word the other kids used: I got a sound spanking for that. But those times of punishment from my father were isolated cases. My chief memories of Prospectville are good—some very good. There was Blackie—in full, Black Beauty, our mixed Shetland and Spanish pony, with one brown eye and one blue eye—and the pony cart Blackie drew. Rides in the pony cart were a staple of the annual Prospectville Country Fair: the red and yellow pony cart is bright in my memory, these sixty years later. (That is *Country* Fair, not *County* Fair—it was organized in Prospectville for Prospectville, I think by my Father and his friends.)

There were our family gatherings, from both families, my mother's and my dad's, in those days. Sometime in the summer, when we were in Prospectville, these family gatherings would have forty to fifty people. We had a large property so there was plenty of room. We had horses so that those who could ride would be able to ride. We had Blackie, the pony, and the pony cart, yellow with red trim. Blackie was very strong and very durable and he could haul twenty-five children in that pony cart—so the picnics at our house were very popular. The children loved those pony rides.

Then there were Georgy David and Stumpy. They were two infant squirrels of the three we rescued when their mother had been killed (by a car or truck perhaps)—they were so young their eyes weren't open. We put them in a shoe box in the oven, to keep them warm, and my mother called the Philadelphia Zoo to find out how to take care of them. The man at the Zoo told her it was hopeless—they wouldn't survive—and she told him she had two children who had rescued them and put them in a shoe box in the oven to keep them warm, and she wasn't going to tell her children that their mother couldn't do anything.

So the man at the Zoo gave her a formula recipe for feeding baby squirrels even though it wasn't going to work and we got a doll-bottle and we nursed those baby squirrels in the dining room, and they survived, and when the man at the Zoo heard about it he said we'd done something no one else had done, at least around Philadelphia. I don't know why we called one Georgy David, but Stumpy was called Stumpy because he had only the stump of a tail.

When we let them go loose, my dad said we'd never see them again, but in the fall they came back and they hung chattering on the screen door to the kitchen, talking to my mother. Dad built a kind of shelf where there was a hole in the tree where they lived (at least I think they lived there). And we used to put food for them there. When Mother hung the laundry out to dry, they would get in the pocket, and Mother would reach in and get them out when she brought the laundry in. But a couple of years later, we were in a hurry to get to the Club so my father could get a swim in before it rained, and Mother got the laundry in and dumped it in the basket, and the squirrels suffocated before we got back. Mother was inconsolable.

When I was a child, especially there in Prospectville, I was extremely active physically, with the riding and the country life: the riding was a great exercise for me. My parents bred German shepherd dogs for the United States Coast Guard "Dogs for Defense" program during the Second World War, and I guess a little after (we had them in Prospectville and we moved there in 1945).

These dogs were great companions for a child like me. I talked to them all the time and we walked around together a lot. We belonged to a country club so I got to swim a lot—which was also good exercise. And one of my joys was to see my father swimming and diving—especially diving—everyone used to stop and watch him dive. (Yes, this may be a point in which my recollections are colored by my "up" mood at the time—though my bipolar condition certainly wasn't fully developed then, and may not have been developed at all.)

If you look up Prospectville, and try to find out what it was like from the last days of World War II, till my father's death in 1954, you'll find some earlier history—that it was a hamlet within Horsham Township, originally called Cashtown, at the intersection of Horsham Road [SR 463] and Limekiln Pike [SR 152], and that it includes Whitemarsh Cemetery—but you won't find much on the years after World War II, when we lived there.

You will also find some references to the Prospectville School, and you will find (after some additional research) that the oldest structure in the hamlet was built, not at the intersection of what are now 463 and 152, but on a high point a little further along Horsham Road (in the opposite direction from the Cemetery). This was a kind of tower-house (almost a blockhouse for defense), where it commanded a view of the road toward Graeme Park [the Keith mansion]: the oldest (stone) part of the house having an 1850s wooden addition. The next owners after us (the Kerpers) built onto the house and it became a general store of a kind. It's still there, adjacent to the big Wawa on the corner, and it currently houses the office of the local state representative.

As I've suggested, I was considered to be on the loud side, whether it was in school, or with my cousins, or later on. I always talked. I was quite often disruptive in school. With my girlfriends, with my cousins, in the family, I spoke out of turn, I bossed, I tattled—"Mommy, daddy hung his bath-towel on the floor." Teachers didn't discipline me as much as they could have because I was a good student. I had the sense—inside me—that I had to speak up because I knew what had to be said—and my mother tended to be that way—she was either singing or talking. I generally wasn't singing—I couldn't really sing.

My non-singing was a great disappointment—to everyone, particularly in my mother's family. My father was quiet; my brother was very quiet. (I remember later on driving with my Uncle Mike (my mother's brother), who had a good voice, and singing along with the car radio and saying, "I wish I could sing, Uncle Mike." He answered, gruffly, "I wish you could too.")

The little school at Prospectville was just down the road from our house. The school was composed of the Music room, the 1st grade room, the 2nd and 3rd grade room and the 4th, 5th, and 6th grade room; the rooms had sliding doors between them. And then downstairs was

8

a lunch room which was also the Cub Scout room and in fact the activities room. We had visitors like state troopers, who came to visit us in that room, and sometimes they brought their dogs. My father started the lunch program through the PTA and he got the bus driver's wife to be the cook and serve the lunches. Lunches were 25 cents apiece and if you didn't have the 25 cents the P.T.A. paid for the lunch. Mrs. Hendry was the lunch lady; Mr. Hendry was the bus driver.

I learned early in life that dogs—and especially in my childhood German Shepherd dogs—are good friends. They are affectionate and they're always there. Horses, on the other hand, for me, don't bring a great deal to the equation. I've ridden horses and enjoyed the experience, and I've known and had friendly horses, but there isn't the kind of intimacy there is with a dog. Even so, I do have wonderful memories of horses, from before my father's death, of riding with my mother and father and my brother Teddy from our house on Horsham Road over to the Keith mansion—the house they call Graeme Park. Graeme Park had been built originally about the same time as the old part of our house, in the mid-1720s, and the houses were just far enough apart and just close enough together for one to have been a kind of outpost for the other—our house for Graeme Park: it was a good ride.

And then my father died.

I think this was what set off my manic depression—if that's possible.

MY FATHER'S DEATH

It went back to a winter day when it was early in the morning, maybe 6 o'clock: he was driving from the house in Prospectville to the greenhouses in Horsham on Witmer Road; it was a blizzard and there was a car in the ditch on the right-hand side of the road and my father got out of his car and lifted the other car out of the ditch, the front end first and then the back end. The car was driven by a registered nurse who worked at the Abington Memorial Hospital and she was on her way to work. He lifted her car back on the road and got her started and then went on his way. He told my mother later that when he lifted the woman's car he felt a pain in his chest. He went to the greenhouses, got the men scheduled to work, and then

the pain increased and he went home and lay down on the couch and the pain kept getting worse. Mother called Dr. Vollmer and he sent an ambulance out to get Daddy to the hospital and they decided he had had a massive heart attack. He was just about forty years old.

That was in February—maybe January—and in April my father was dead. He never recovered from the heart attack; he was sent home from the hospital and he kept trying to get out of bed. He was never without pain and I was thinking, when I started looking at my memories, that he never left the second floor of the house. But that wasn't true: he had one time he went to the greenhouses, and they told my mother after he died that he had been potting orchids and told them not to tell my mother. He had been a very heavy smoker and eaten a lot of pork roast and gravy—but was a very active athlete.

He played football when he was younger, I think for the Frankford Yellow-jackets, which had been a predecessor of the Philadelphia Eagles, and then become a semi-pro team. (I also remember a team called the Springfield Green-jackets.)

He was also a swimmer and a diver, and played golf, and ice hockey. I remember he was always very fit—until this. Sometime after his death, when mother and Uncle Tom and the family were talking about my dad, and they couldn't understand how he was such a terrific athlete but he died so quickly, they decided it must have been financial stress, trying to make it on his own in growing orchids and roses, separate from Uncle Bill. Later on, my Aunt Doris told me the reason my father didn't make money was because of my mother's wild spending—a fur coat when he should have been putting the money back in the business. And she actually had two fur coats.

I guess much of it was stress. But it wasn't just stress, I think. When my dad was born [in 1913] he was what they called a blue baby—meaning he had a bad heart. And when he was a little boy he always had something wrong. He built himself up over the years—I was told later by aunts or uncles that all he wanted to do was play football. One of his uncles [on his mother's side] was one of the owners of the Grace Lines, and my grandfather talked Uncle Phil into having Daddy work as a stoker in the boiler room—before he went to college. He worked two years on the Grace Lines.

The second year he brought home a baby ocelot that he gave to the Brooklyn zoo—he hated to part with him because he loved that ocelot and used to carry him around like a kitten but my grandmother wouldn't have an ocelot in the house. The second year he was on the ship he hurt his leg and it was very bad; they cruised up to California to an American hospital and they were going to take his leg off.

My grandmother took the train out to California and talked the doctors out of taking his leg off but he didn't get to play as much football as he wanted. He also had a bad eye—I guess (I was very young then)—and they had to put injections into his eye at the Wills Eye Hospital. (He told us that on the trip that ended in California the stokers on the ship used to sit on the floor playing poker and nobody spoke the same language and everyone had a knife.)

I think, looking back on it, he really didn't have enough strength to lift that car. Fourteen years before, he had had a ruptured appendix and was in an oxygen tent and they didn't think he was going to pull through—this was after he married my mother in 1939 and before I was born in 1941. He had a kidney condition too. But he was my daddy and I knew he was strong, and until I looked back while we were writing this I didn't recall all the weaknesses and problems. He was always very trim. And on the morning when my brother came to my room and said "Daddy's dying—you better come see him!" I didn't believe him and I didn't go right away.

YOUTH AFTER DADDY'S DEATH: FLOWERS TO FLIGHT

What happened to me when he died? You know, I was reading a memoir by C. S. Lewis the other day, and he talks about the effect of his mother's death when he was a child: "With my mother's death [he wrote], all settled happiness, all that was tranquil and reliable, disappeared from my life. There was to be much fun, many pleasures, many stabs of Joy; but no more of the old security. It was sea and islands now; the great continent had sunk like Atlantis." And C. S. Lewis, so far as I know, wasn't even a manic depressive. But he has hit it off pretty exactly here for what happened to me, when my father died.

Of course, I remember the greenhouses, from before my father's death—and after—of course, after. I remember looking at the orchids—mostly brown and green orchids—in the orchid greenhouse. I can still see them in my mind's eye—and all the roses in the other greenhouses. My husband asked me just now if my dad had other flowers besides roses and orchids—I don't think so—just some highly specialized orchids. I believe he and Uncle Bill developed a rose that was a predecessor to the American Beauty rose—the Better Times rose—they did it for someone else so he could take the proceeds from it. This was at the end of the Depression and before we went to Prospectville.

I can see the gravel walkways, the wooden walkways, the cistern that held water for the greenhouses—it had frogs in it and my brother used to come down and get the frogs. I can look at each greenhouse in my memory—the orchid houses with the shelves for all the orchids. I can see the greenhouses for the roses—roses as high as I was—white, red, yellow, pink, and a color called talisman—like a yellow orange.

White, yellow, pink, red—my dad's favorite was a red, my mother's was yellow, mine was pink—Teddy didn't have a favorite that I know of—the only thing he liked about the greenhouses was the frogs from the cistern. And there was one other color I remember in thinking about the roses—but not the color of any rose. In preparing roses for market we had to cut them and sort them by size, and then we wrapped them with white wax paper. Printed on the wax paper in large letters in dark green was "Roses by Starke" [Edward P. Starke, Hatboro, Pennsylvania].

Of course the orchids were all colors and they were exquisite—they were shipped all over the world—the United States, Hawaii, Britain—Hawaii wasn't a state then—and every greenhouse had hoses because everything had to be watered. And of course the shed was where we packed—put the orchids in glass tubes and we put the roses in white wrappers. In the center of the houses for the orchids was a potting shed where my father potted all the orchids. At that time they were potted in peat moss and osmunda fiber.

If you wonder about osmunda fiber—it isn't used much now—it's the stuff, including some of the fern itself, from around where osmunda ferns grow. It was used a lot for orchids in those days. My father was the only one who potted. It was believed it contributed to his death because the fibers got into his lungs. He was also the only one who put the cut orchids in the glass tubes. His orchids and my Uncle Bill's orchids were considered the best around. Starke crosses were started in glass tubes with cotton and the little orchid seeds.

It was understood between my father and my Uncle Bill that if either of them died, the crosses would go to the other. But my mother hated Daddy's family and she wouldn't abide by the agreement—much to our financial distress.

An "orchid cross" is an orchid cross-bred from two different lines of orchids—what might be called a hybrid. Most named orchids now in existence are "crosses." My father and his brother developed many orchid crosses, including the Naomi Starke (for my Aunt Nomy—Uncle Bill's wife), the Anne Starke Atkinson (for their sister, my Aunt Anne), the Jane Elizabeth Starke (for me), the William Clark Mason, the Isabelle Henderson, the Hal Patterson, the Walter Winchell—the William Clark Mason won an award. They also developed rose crosses, too, including the Good Times.

YOUTH/YOUNG ADULTHOOD: WORK AND A YOUNG MAN

As I said, I was almost thirteen when my dad died and things made their great huge shift (or maybe I should say the world shifted and I began to). Mother began to drink, later becoming a full-blown alcoholic. My brother went to the Milton Hershey School for Boys. And I was taken out of school at thirteen to work in my father's greenhouses until they were sold. I worked seven days a week with nine Italian rose-growers—they had worked for my dad for many years and they were extremely kind to me.

They showed me everything from pulling hoses to cutting roses. I learned how to sort, bunch, ice, and pack huge boxes of roses. I couldn't lift the boxes to put them in the station wagon. They had to do the lifting. They taught me how to drive and at thirteen I drove station-wagon-load after station-wagon-load of beautiful flowers to wholesalers in Philadelphia and buses in Willow Grove from which they were bussed all over the United States. (With no driver's license, barely able to reach the pedals.)

I was responsible for negotiating the prices with the wholesalers. I also did the payroll. I learned fast. I don't know how it happened but I was never stopped by a policeman, though I drove from thirteen to sixteen without a license; I was never arrested. I had to sit on a cushion and had pedals on top of the pedals.

Uncle Tom taught me payroll procedures—at the greenhouses—he was my mother's next-to-oldest brother, eight years older than my mother, three years older than my father. Uncle Tom was married to Aunt Rose. Aunt Rose was considered to be extremely beautiful—and she died of cancer when my cousin Stephanie was three. Uncle Tom was traveling for the IRS all over the United States and he left Stevie with my mother—his sister. Stevie remembers my mother singing while driving and pumping the gas pedal with the music. She also remembers my mother yelling and screaming—is there a clue there? (Is there a clue in my mother's spending?)

I worked night and day at the greenhouses, and I often came home to being by myself. The arrangement was that I would stay there until the greenhouses were sold. There were fourteen greenhouses, 50,000 square feet under glass, and selling them was a large order. They were coal-stokers except for one and they were hard to heat. I also learned to drive the tractor so I could take the coal and put it into the coal-stokers. When my Uncle Mike was there he drove the tractor and took care of the coal-stokers for me but he wasn't always there.

And there was a young man named Hugh—I guess he was sixteen or seventeen, a couple of years older than I was—who lived down the road, but he was a friend of my Cousin Buddy, off at the school they went to. (Buddy was my Aunt May and Uncle Bud's younger son and youngest child—he was a Starke cousin—and he was my best and favorite dance partner.) Hugh would sometimes help me with the stokers.

He had a car, a convertible, and I would call him for help, and he would say, "Janie, I've got better things to do than come over to help you with the stokers." And I would say, "Can't you pretend you don't have better things to do?" and he would come over and help me. Then the greenhouses were sold and I heaved a sigh of relief only to have that sale fall through. Hugh went away into the U. S. Coast Guard—he loved boats—and by the time he came back, we didn't have the greenhouses any more.

When my mother started drinking, my own drinking picked up with hers. She drank at home and in bars and I drank with her, and followed her into bars. She may not have been bipolar, but she was violent. And she never went a day without drinking—and by this time neither did I. I remember being out on a date and coming home and my mother wasn't home which was very rare: she was usually sitting in the chair drinking. I heard this yelling and had no idea who or what it was—and I put my head out the window and it was my mother yelling, "Janie I've just been 'bucky bathing' ['bucky' as in 'buck naked'] at the Buck's [friends of hers with their own swimming pool]"—I was mortified. She broadcast it all over the neighborhood.

The College Settlement Farm Camp was next to the greenhouses. It was managed by the Philadelphia Quakers. In the summer, students from Germantown Friends School, one of the Quaker schools in Philadelphia, worked at College Settlement, took care of the children, and taught them swimming, baseball, and all that. That's where I met my friend Betsy and her younger brother Louis, who was about eight months older than I was.

Louis and I got along splendidly and I had a huge crush on him. Our friendship lasted through his college years and after. After my second divorce, Louis temporarily re-entered my life, and again it was a wonderful friendship despite my difficulties.

One of Louis's uncles was the head of Columbia Records and he gave Louis all kinds of tickets to all kinds of entertainment, and Louis's favorite—and mine—was Louis Armstrong. (By the way, just as Louis Armstrong was Lou-is not Lou-ie, so was my friend Lou-is.) We saw Louis Armstrong at Sunnybrook, and in New York City, and several times at the Newport Jazz Festival. We used to go back in his dressing room. I guess it was obvious to him that we suffered from Louis Armstrong hero worship, and he was very kind to us.

Once, Louis's family was vacationing in Nantucket and I was invited. I think I was 16—and I had nothing to wear, really nothing. But my mother had a friend who was the manager of the local Peck & Peck store, and she outfitted me from the store with outfits for the whole two weeks in Nantucket. I was dressed so well I felt like a million bucks every time I put on a new outfit. The whole time on Nantucket was like a voyage in another world. I can still see the yachts in the harbor—one huge yacht in particular—I'd never seen a yacht that size.

When I got back from the trip I gave Jean all my clothes. She had them dry-cleaned and put back in the store, and so far as I know, to this day (more than half a century later) no one found out. It was a magic time. I saw things—and people—I had never expected to see, except in pictures. And I was part of it and I was dressed as part of it.

YOUTH AND YOUNG ADULT: THE GREENHOUSES

Then thank God! (I said to myself), the greenhouses were sold for good. But my joy (if that's what it was) was short-lived.

Not only had I missed all that school and I had to go about earning a living with no education—but we had moved up to Bethlehem, Pennsylvania, away from places I knew, closer to my mother's family, and she opened a dance studio. Unfortunately the dance studio was a partnership and my mother was cheated by her partner, and times were very bad.

My mother rented the studio from Nick, who owned a bar downstairs and this huge room upstairs. The Dance Studio went under and my mother was very sick. Nick gave me food to take home for her and me. I can remember I used to go down and go into the restaurant and into the bar, as there was a counter there, and I didn't even have to ask him, and he would say "How's your mother?" and I would say "Still in bed," and he would give me a huge plate of spaghetti and meatballs, and cover it with something, and then he would say "Don't forget to come back tomorrow." She was so sick I had to spoon feed her and she couldn't eat very much at all.

She had two things wrong. One of them was some kind of burns on her eyes from sitting under a sunlamp. She was in a lot of pain— very sick with that—and at the same time she had real bad flu—and it was worse because she had lost every dime she had and had lost the business. And she still owed rent, though Nick wasn't collecting it.

When she recovered, we moved. Mother's friend moved us to an apartment in Chestnut Hill and that's when I got the job as a girl Friday, and my mother got a job in Philadelphia in advertising. I don't know if all these ups and downs and unexpected relief out of despair had any part in developing my bipolar life pattern, but I suppose it's possible. Real life seemed to be mimicking the manic-depressive patterns.

And then, after the job in advertising, my mother got the job at the nursing home in Chestnut Hill. Then (a few years later) she opened her own retirement home in rented buildings (on the old Thayer estate). After a number of years there in Gwynedd Valley she opened another home—under the old name—in Montgomeryville.

This time she owned the property. From the days at her first "Blue Skies" her course of life was set. Mine took longer to set—if indeed it has, even now.

Fortunately I was attractive and had good legs. My first job was modeling bathing suits: I was Miss Cape Coral Florida. I never went to Cape Coral—never been there in my life. I wore a black bathing suit, fishnet, and very high heels. Although I looked very good I didn't make a lot of money. Then I got my job with Mr. D. as a Girl Friday. I didn't know what a Girl Friday was at that time.

About getting that job—I had to lie to Mr. D.—you see, I really didn't know how to do anything. I had to learn how to type and I went to night school. I taught myself how to type and take dictation. Mr. D. asked me—when he heard me typing so slowly—if I misrepresented myself on my application and I said yes. That's when he told me if I took a course offered at a local high-school—it may have been Upper Dublin—and learned typing and bookkeeping and A-B-C shorthand, the company would pay for it and I did and they did. Meanwhile I did those letters the way I did and they were perfect, though slow.

YOUNG ADULT FINALLY—FLYING

My next job was with a major airline recently in the headlines, and I think that's where I began to become an adult—a very young one. Once again I looked good and had a good time, but didn't make much money. I probably was under age—I was twenty—and my height was borderline (though once I was hired I did stretching exercises which brought me up to five foot four—sort of), and I didn't have the necessary high-school diploma. But I was hired.

I boarded a flight at Philadelphia and went out to Chicago, changed planes in Chicago for Frontier Airlines. I was on a DC-3 and it was the noisiest thing I was ever on, and I flew into Cheyenne, Wyoming. At Cheyenne I was taken out to the air base and we trained there, in a big warehouse. We ate in the barracks with the military and we were the only females. We had all our meals there, and then we went into our barracks and we had our sleeping quarters and classrooms and training. We found out while we were in this training that we were the last class the airline would have in Cheyenne. Afterwards they were all to be in Chicago, where they were even to have a swimming pool. We were pretty upset about that.

I remember Cheyenne Days right after we finished our course—they had the cattle coming through the streets, with all the dust, and cowboys with chaps and bandannas and hats. It was tremendously exciting. Of course everybody knew who we were. They were buying us beers but I had a ginger ale. We got Cheyenne wooden nickels—I still may have one. We had been in stewardess training five-and-a-half weeks, the longest of any training for any line. I don't know if that's still the case. Then we went to Denver where we stayed at the Brown Palace Hotel and were sworn in. Then we left for our domiciles—mine was Minneapolis. So I lived in Minneapolis, which of course is (or at least was then) one of the loveliest cities ever—beautifully clean. I loved it.

I lived with three other gals in a special apartment building for airline employees who were in and out of town. We got along pretty well when we were there together—but a couple of times, either because I was drunk, or because I was manic, or both, they put me under the covers in bed to keep me there. (I had forgotten about this for fifty years till it came out as I was writing—or rather dictating—just now.) There was a real nice fellow and we had dinner in Denver and he said come up to my hotel so I walked up and we got to the door and he started to unbutton my stewardess blouse and I looked at him and said I don't think so—he asked why—I said "I changed my mind"—and I left. Was that bi-polar behavior? Well, you see, I don't know what I'd said before.

I regularly flew Minneapolis to Chicago to Denver and loved the run. One night I went to pick up my flight and the despatcher would not let me board. He said I had bronchitis and if I got sick I could sue the airline. I was furious—I had a flying lesson scheduled in Denver—but dispatchers have the law. I went back to the apartment I shared with the other gals. He was right. I didn't feel well. And I laid down on the couch and in no time I was sound asleep.

At 11 p.m. I was wakened by the phone. It was my mother. My plane had crashed in Denver. Now I have remembered for years that most of the passengers were killed, but in the records I've checked, that wasn't the case. According to these records, Flight 859 crashed on landing in Denver [at Stapleton] and burned, with 121 on board [seven crew-members]. Seventeen passengers died and one person on the ground, sixteen from smoke inhalation and carbon monoxide poisoning.

All 104 living passengers were taken to the hospital. It was a failure of the hydraulic system during a landing emergency [the flaps failed to extend properly], and some blame attached to the first officer for failure to monitor the gauges correctly when applying reverse thrust. But I remember my escape from death as being narrower than the figures I've looked up suggest

That crash I missed was the end of my flying career, except that I had a couple more flights before I came home. Everybody was on the phone calling me, aunts and uncles, and I was back at home in almost no time. My mother was supposed to meet me at the Airport. (My flight home was a deadhead, as I was neither working the flight nor paying for it—I guess it was my last flight for the Airline.) No, I don't believe anyone was forced to leave my plane to release that seat for me. That wasn't how things were done fifty-five years ago.

When I got to the Airport in Philadelphia my mother wasn't there. She said on the phone, when I called her, "Get a cab!" I got a cab and the cabbie was friendly and chatty—his big news was that Philadelphia now allowed beer in the ballpark and he thought it was about time. (I had no opinion—I didn't go to baseball games and I didn't like beer—but I was glad the cabbie was happy.) When I got home, my mother gave me a check to pay the cabdriver. Surprisingly he took it without any complaints.

I never quite understood and still don't quite understand how I got the airlines job without the high-school diploma. They gave me tests and I did well, and I was very good-looking. Maybe that explains it all. I don't quite understood how I got that job, and I don't quite understand how I got my job at the space company. I had a lot of tests both places, and apparently I did well.

When I got back home, I asked the supervisor if there were any ground jobs in Philadelphia. She called and found out there weren't any at that time, but she said I should keep on checking. I tried several times at the airline desk at Philadelphia airport but there was nothing available and they kept saying please try again—please try again. Meanwhile, my previous employer—Mr. D.—had called my mother to see how I was doing. They had hired someone to replace me and she didn't work out.

So they asked me to return to my old job, which I did, I worked there for several years after that.

FIRST MARRIAGE, THEN THE SNAKE PIT, A BRIEF INTERLUDE, AND THEN…

Not long after that, my friend Hugh—my cousin Buddy's friend—had come back from the Coast Guard, and I think just about the first thing he did was, he called Janie on the phone. We began dating and we got along very well, and we got married. (His mother, by the way, had been my father's high-school teacher—there was that earlier connection of a sort.) This was the first example of my not being cut out for marriage. As nice as he was—and though he had experience with my demands before—he found it very hard to deal with me, and we were divorced after less than two years.

He divorced me after my suicide attempt but that was not the only reason—I was very unreasonable in lots of ways. There isn't much I can say about this marriage. I loved him—I think—but I'm not sure I really had any idea what love was about. It was a big church wedding, but there was no one there from my family—my mother had cut ties with my father's family, and she didn't want to come, so her family didn't. That's about all I can say about the first marriage—except that Hugh got along very well with my mother.

And, especially, I got along very well with his parents. I called them "Dad" and "Moth" (that isn't the word "moth"—it's the first syllable of "Mother"). They were rich—both of them had Jaguars—was it a Mark 10 and Mark 8?—that Dad had bought in England and had shipped over. Moth didn't really like hers—she liked her big blue ['62?] T-bird. His Jag was a stick—hers was an automatic, but she never drove it anyway. Hers had a radio—his didn't—he never put radios in his cars—even "Milly," their Fiat, didn't have a radio. In those days Jaguar owners needed back-up cars, and that was what Milly was.

When I was married to his son, Dad (remember, he was my first father-in-law) and I would go out driving in his Jaguar on Sunday afternoons. He would tell me where to go. My husband didn't want to drive his father—he would spend Sunday afternoons either at the Firehouse or working for his friend Carl—and Moth and Claire (my sister-in-law) couldn't drive stick. Dad and I went sailing too, on his Day-Sailor. No one else wanted to go with him.

The day-sailor was a new class in those days—it was and I think still is 16' 9" long and 6' 3" in the beam—just about the smallest boat for more than one passenger, though two in a day-sailor may be quite enough.) And after my husband divorced me, I still went sailing and driving with Dad, though not as often, because I wasn't there as much.

I got a new job, wearing high heels and fishnet stockings and a red velvet and gold lamé (very brief costume) in a "gay nineties" style (no, that's the *old* meaning of "gay") in three rebuilt classic railroad cars outside of Fort Washington. First I was a hatcheck girl, and I learned how to manage the dish with the quarters in it—not too many quarters and right under my eye), and then I graduated to bringing drinks. I didn't really enjoy the job, but the money rolled in and I would deposit the cash in a nearby bank—not in a checking account. I didn't even know how a checking account worked. So I took $1800 in cash and bought a new blue 1965 Mustang at the Ford dealer. I was "up"—and he was amazed. Then I quit my job. Andy, the boss, was not happy—and I was not thinking ahead.

I loved that car. And then ...

CALL IT A SNAKE PIT

I found myself in a small examining room with a large black woman in a white uniform. She told me to take off all my clothes, bend over, and touch my toes. When I did that, she checked my rectum—I think it was with her hand. I didn't know what was going on, but later found out she was looking for drugs. She checked my vagina and then of course my mouth and ears, my underarms, and under my breasts.

She then gave me a packet which contained hospital clothes, under-panties, a sleeveless undershirt, a dress, and sneaker-type shoes. I was taken into the ward. This was at nighttime. I couldn't really see very well. I was given a bed with one blanket and one pillow and when I was left alone I was approached. The entire time I was to stay there I was approached frequently, and the approaches usually were composed of groping—groping my breasts, my vagina, my butt.

I may have been the youngest gal there and obviously came from "better circumstances" (or they thought I did). Other patients frequently tried to get my attention one way or another. I was finally put in the suicide watch—I had gone into the hospital because of a suicide attempt—the suicide watch was a crib next to the nurses' station, under a ceiling light. I was terrified. I was tired. I was scared. I had a light shining in my eyes and I couldn't sleep no matter how much I wanted to.

The next morning I was taken into a big arena with doctors and nurses—it was called Staffing—and they asked me a million questions. They wanted to know why I razor-bladed my arms. Did I really want to die? Or was I just looking for attention? I was insulted by their questions and by their manner—their attitude. I said that I was sincere. They asked me when I left the hospital: would I do it again? I told them I didn't know—by the way I never have done it again.

They must have thought I was sincere enough (whatever that was) in the answers I gave—because, after three days, they let me go. But I was considered hostile because, when they asked me my first name, I said "Mrs." I forgot to mention that the women walked around and went to the bathroom in trash cans. There were no faucet-handles on the sinks, only buttons you pushed. There were no mirrors, only pieces of steel. Buttons on the toilets too.

And if you went to tell the staff someone was pooping in the trash can, they were so overwhelmed with the difficulties in that unit, they didn't pay attention. If you told them the other patients grabbed your breasts or anything else, they wouldn't acknowledge. I guess they couldn't acknowledge. They didn't have the ability to solve the horrible problems existing in this Snake Pit, even if they wanted to solve them, which—looking way back—I think they probably did. (I didn't think so then—it's hard for me to bring back my overwhelming fear, dislike, anger of those days—though probably not hard enough.)

All the time you were there you were not allowed outside. There was almost no outside for the patients. There were almost no windows. Everyone was out of the space they belonged in. The staff had no idea where to begin, regarding any problems. And the patients were so overwhelmed with their problems that all that happened with them—the problems—was that they magnified as they went along.

A year later I found myself in a luxurious private hospital. I was there because I couldn't stop crying and no one knew why—

including me. I was put in this hospital and the first thing they did was give me truth serum. They gave me two or three other drugs that were designed to open you up and bring out whatever was in your head. Nothing worked. I continued to cry all the time. So then they gave me some other drugs, thinking they would calm me and maybe ease the crying. But they didn't work either.

Before they started the treatment they gave me an injection of something like valium or librium so I would calm down before they gave me the treatment. I don't think it worked. I remember being hysterical and really afraid and then I was unconscious—completely out.

Then Dr. Bell decided to give me electroshock treatments, and they started me on those. [I think the technical name is Electroconvulsive Therapy—ECT.] The way they worked, you got a treatment three times a week and the treatments and the breaks in between were designed to calm the patient. They didn't work. The doctor was just beside himself. I was so young—that was one thing. Three ECT treatments a week for six weeks—eighteen altogether and after the shock treatment you had no memory at all—no memory— my family would come to see me and I didn't know who they were and then another day later another treatment and any memory I was beginning to get back would go. These treatments were considered bi-hemispheric—both hemispheres of the head.

By that time I was twenty-two (and a half) and nothing was working. I had gotten eighteen of the double-hemisphere electro- shock treatments and I was still crying. Not only was I still crying and didn't know why, but I didn't recognize anyone in my family either. They were extremely distraught after spending three or four months and a huge amount of money—and grateful that the tab was picked up by my father's estate (from the sale of the greenhouses). But I was just as sick as I had been.

I left the private hospital at the end of the shock treatments and all I did was cry—so my mother went over to the state hospital at Norristown to see Dr. Michael Maguire. She tried to explain to him what was going on with me, and could he please get me well. He agreed to take me into the hospital on the Cadre Program where I was given lots of physical activity and sunshine and fresh air. My mother said "Doctor, she's so sick—please give her some medicine."

He said, "Mrs. S-----, I know your daughter is very sick but she's also very young and I cannot give her medicine." My mother didn't understand that at all, but the doctor said he believed that course of therapy would help me. He was right. It did. It was in the summer and I had a lot of wonderful weather and wonderful days to be outside. By the way, part of the therapy was mopping the women's dormitory room every morning, and drying the dishes after every meal. After three or four months Dr. Maguire said I could leave.

While I was there at Norristown State Hospital, a well-known artist from Philadelphia was in the same section I was in. She did a charcoal portrait of me which, half a century later (almost), is framed and hanging in our living room. (It's also reproduced in this book: it gives no current clues to my identity.) When I got out I couldn't go to my mother's because she was so abusive physically. So I got permission to go stay with my Aunt Doris in Bethlehem. Aunt Doris was married to my Uncle Rich, my mother's middle brother; they had no children. She was an alcoholic and of course I was an alcoholic—at least a budding alcoholic (maybe "blooming" would be better)—but there was no abuse and we got along very well.

I had to go to see the doctor every two weeks and I had no transportation. So my father-in-law—actually by then my ex-father-in-law but I still called him "Dad"—had several cars including the Fiat "Milly"—which I was more than grateful to have. But one night I went out with friends to a saloon somewhere and when I came out several hours later "Milly" wasn't there.

I called my father-in-law and told him what happened and he and everyone he knew searched high and low for the Fiat. It never re-appeared. I have never felt that I apologized adequately for losing Milly. At that time of my life, my [ex-] father-in-law was probably the only person in the world who would lend me anything, particularly a car, and I have never been able to explain what happened to it.

And then...

THE SALEM INTERLUDE

There is quite a lot for me to say about the "and then" part. When I was divorced and not yet remarried and trying to live a life of pleasant recreation—after the "Snake Pit" interlude and the time when I lost "Milly"—I swam every chance I got and I loved to sail. It was at about this time I met another fellow—his name was David—and we used to travel together and one day he said, "Jane let's go up to New York and check out a boat for sale." So we did. We went to Montauk and saw the most beautiful antique teak vessel imaginable. He said to me "Do you want to take a spin?" I said "Sure."

That boat was just lovely, brass fittings, teak wood, and we took a cruise up to Marblehead, Massachusetts, where he said he had some friends. The owner was nowhere around but we weren't deterred. We cruised up to Marblehead. Then, up in Massachusetts, I was taken—I was unconscious—and put on a kind of plank held up in the air in the woods as for an altar—this was right near Marblehead (maybe, looking back, it was in the Witch-ground of Salem)—and everyone got together and lit candles in the woods.

There must have been about twenty people. The candles were huge—I remember that. The people had me up on this altar and I woke up and found myself with candles all around and I didn't have any clothes on and my jewelry was stolen, my gold charm bracelet, and then they took me down off that altar. I must have been given some kind of a drink or something. I certainly didn't take my clothes off myself (that I know of). I remember the candles all around when I woke up—or came to, one of those things—and I was terrified.

I left with the two guys I was with, and my friend and I and the other man made it back to the boat where we were docked at Marblehead. I don't remember whether anyone else came back to the boat. I don't think so.

We began our cruise back down the east coast of the United States, I think it was the next day. I was pretty quiet on the boat for the next two days—I didn't really know where I'd been or what I'd done or what had been done to me. We had beautiful weather and the water was perfect. We were somewhere off the coast of Maryland when we were boarded by the United States Coast Guard and I was terrified. We were arrested for stealing the boat. They told me this. I was arrested and I was being held by the United States Coast Guard and I couldn't go anywhere. I told them that I didn't steal the boat; I was just a passenger. I had been gone from home a long time—I may have been gone a couple of months and my mother didn't know where I was.

MY BROTHER TO THE RESCUE!

But when we were arrested I called my brother and he must (almost) have flown down from Philadelphia (actually he drove). When he told the Coast Guard he had to return me to the State Hospital where I was a patient, they were flabbergasted. He told them he could return me after the hospital checked me out—I had to be there every two or three weeks.

They told my brother he could take me back to the hospital and after I had been checked out he could bring me back for trial. We left. The ride home was pretty difficult—my brother kept yelling at me for being so stupid. I noticed I never heard from the Coast Guard. I said to my brother one day "Did you ever hear from the Coast Guard?" He said no, he hadn't. I said "Why do you think that is?" He said, "Sister, I just don't think they want to deal with this crazy blonde, who is really certified crazy." To this very day I have never heard again from the United States Coast Guard—nor did my brother to the day of his death. I didn't see David after that either, but nearly ten years later he was killed in a plane crash in Vermont and I was notified because I was still on his list of emergency contacts.

MY BROTHER

My relationship with my brother was not always as good as it was at the time of the "borrowed" boat (even though he was really angry with me then). There was one time when you might say we were at opposite ends of a car—his car. It was at a family party at my mother's—only my mother's family—at the time when I was married to my second husband. My brother was very fond of pickled eggs and I had made up a big batch just for him. When I put them on the table he said their color wasn't very good, and I pushed the eggs firmly in his direction. I didn't hit him with them—even though it may have been suggested I did—I just pushed them very firmly at him. He picked up a huge picnic table. My husband held him down and told me to get out—I ran out to get into a car.

The only car I could see unlocked and that had keys in it was my brother's brand new Firebird. So I got in and started down the road. My brother was running right by me and I ran over him. At least he was now on the road behind the car. Then apparently I ran over him again. I don't know how it happened but there wasn't a mark on him anywhere. Somebody got my brother's car away from me and my husband took me home. My brother was understandably enraged—but all I could think of was there wasn't a mark on him. I apologized. I was terribly sorry I had done that. I didn't know what got into me.

But he wouldn't accept my apology. Several years later after an A. A. meeting (when we were both sober) my brother came up to me and said I had never apologized to him for running over him. I said I had; he said it didn't count because I was still drinking when I apologized, so I had to apologize all over again, so I did. (He was right—I really hadn't made a felt apology—just words). After all this happened at the family party—or outside it—someone remarked my mother was missing from the party.

Someone went and found her upstairs with a shotgun between her toes and she was going to shoot herself. She didn't know what she'd done to deserve such children. With perfect timing, just then a policeman walked in (perhaps someone had called the police). The cop was someone who had worked part-time for my dad fifteen or twenty years before, so he knew my mother—and he said, "Kay, you don't really want to kill yourself."

She said she did, and he said "Kay, just come downstairs and talk it over"—and she did, so we still had a mother. She couldn't hold the shot gun with her fingers and have it at her head at the same time. It was a Scott family show and everyone—except the cop—was drunk.

So here I was—a single gal who had spent some time as Miss Cape Coral [Florida]—but no time in Cape Coral. Now I had my job working in the nightclub in Fort Washington, wearing that extremely abbreviated costume, more or less on the order of the playboy bunny type. I worked so hard five or six nights a week and made so much money that I bought that dark-blue and white-top Mustang convertible and paid that cash for it.

MEETING MR. G

My next job after the nightclub was with an employment agency and then came the interview with the large missile and space corporation in the Philadelphia area. Once again I didn't have the "book" qualifications—I didn't have a high-school diploma. Not only that—I had already been in Dufour Hospital and had all those shock treatments. I was afraid they'd find out about the diploma I didn't have and the shock treatments I did have. They didn't. I did well on the tests and they called Mr. G. and told him I had done well on the tests, and he hired me.

Being able to test out very well—and to lie very well (phony birth date and age, high-school diploma—all that) —and being blonde and having good legs—all went together to get jobs. Maybe that was all there was to it—except I think I got the jobs on the upswing when I was full of self-confidence, perhaps to a manic point. I didn't know there was anything wrong with this lying—I had to do what I had to do in order to get the job. And the job I got back after the airline was another example. I was obviously a quick learner—don't know whether that had anything to do with being on an upswing in my cycle—I'm not sure I ever took on this kind of thing when I was down. But remember, I didn't really know about any cycles I might have.

You remember that when I got out of Norristown State Hospital I couldn't go to my mother's because she was physically abusive. So I got permission to go stay with my Aunt Doris in Bethlehem. Eventually I left Aunt Doris's and I'd made enough money to get a little house. There was an auction place in Norristown—I loved the auctions—and that was mostly how I furnished that little house. (I loved the excitement of the auction, and I think I got some pretty good bargains.)

But the house didn't have central heating, and from the summer when I moved in, through most of the winter, it was heated with this kerosene heater I'd bought. The kerosene heater comes into my story a little later on. Right now, I'm reflecting, it was a kinder gentler time back then. Mr. Hoey—I think that was his name—would deliver five dollars' worth of kerosene for the heater. I would leave my door unlocked when he was going to deliver, and I would leave the check for five dollars there, and he would bring the kerosene in for the heater, and fill it, and take the check, and go on his rounds, and that would be that.

Anyway (to shift gears back again), Mr. G. at the space company hired me as his secretary. He would send me over to the main building where the top executives had their huge offices. When I would pull over, I would see whose parking space was empty, and I would pull in there. I would go into the building and do whatever business I had to do—deliver papers, get papers, or whatever.

I would go out and get into the car and go back to the building where I worked and I thought no one was the wiser. No one ever said a word. I did that three or four or five times and every time was just as smooth as could be, until the last time, and then two of the guards came after me and they called to me and I didn't say anything—I just kept on walking fast—and then they pulled their guns, and when they pulled their guns I moved that car as fast as I could and I got back to my building, thinking it was just one event, and otherwise, no one was the wiser.

I had no idea how they figured it out but they knew who I was and they called my boss. They told him if I ever did that again I wouldn't be working there. He was unhappy, I was terrified, but I never did it again. Whenever I went over to the main building I parked as far away as I could and walked carefully into the main building, and then did whatever I was there to do.

NEW BEGINNINGS (ADULTHOOD, SOBRIETY, SANITY): SECOND MARRIAGE.

I started dating Mr. G. At first I was very leery of letting him know where I lived, so I had him drop me off where my friend Harriet and her husband Brook lived. Then, finally, I got up my courage and had him take me to my little house. He came in with me, and I turned on the kerosene heater. He was horrified.

He told me I would blow myself up or burn the house down or both. He got me an apartment in Philadelphia that had real heat—central heating. We were married about eight or nine months later, and he moved into the apartment with me while our house was being built. I think there was a policy about working in the same department married, and I left my job. I went to work at a nursery as a bookkeeper.

My husband was quite handy around the house. When he was married to his first wife (I still sent her a birthday card every year until she died a few years ago), he had bought some buildings in partnership with her mother ("Mom-mom"), and—with two college degrees—he had gone to night school at a Philadelphia high school to learn plumbing and carpentry, and electrical work—everything you needed to keep buildings in order. Very handy around our house. Very handy around my mother's retirement house, Blue Skies (more on that later).

Sometime after that, my husband obtained custody of his two daughters, ages nine or ten and one and a half. I very much loved being a stepmother but I still had trouble being married. Sometimes I had trouble as a stepmother too. I remember screaming at my older stepdaughter—she was thirteen—humiliating her in front of her friends. (I don't know whether the screaming came from alcohol or from mania—but I knew immediately I had humiliated her and I apologized. The difficulty was, it was already done.) My second husband was instrumental in both getting me to A. A. and on lithium. We were married nine years. Eventually his first wife regained custody of the children, despite her being schizophrenic.

My first exposure to A. A. in 1969 had been about six meetings in Moorestown, New Jersey—six meetings (there might have been seven) where I was unable to identify as an alcoholic, where I came as late as I could, and left as early as I could, and just wanted to get out of there. (This seems to have been in a "down" period in my "cyclothymic" illness.) Whatever my problems were (and I didn't think they were as bad as my husband did), I knew a group of drunks just couldn't help me—the best psychiatrists had already failed. And I didn't exactly get to A. A. on my own that time. It wasn't my idea.

I was at the shore with my two stepdaughters and my mother, and I was to pick up my husband at the Philadelphia airport. I never arrived at the airport, and to this day I have no idea where I went: I simply forgot I was supposed to pick him up. When he got down to the shore, I was out somewhere with my brother. I had left the children in my mother's care—my mother who was a serious alcoholic—and my husband was furious. My trip to the shore was cut short—very short, immediately, and not by me.

When we got home, my husband called A. A.—the South Jersey Intergroup—and they asked if he would put his wife on the phone. I got on the phone and the person on the other end asked me if I had a drinking problem. I told them I didn't know, but my husband thought I did. They asked me my first name and phone number. Within twelve minutes I had a call from the lady who eventually (a year later) became my first sponsor. (It turned out she lived within sight of my house.) But you know, as far as I was concerned, I wasn't like these people. Or not yet! But why did it work the next year? Was it simply cyclothymic timing? Was it the effects of a dream I had the last night I drank?

My last drinking weekend began on Friday, October 2, 1970, in Moorestown, New Jersey. I drove to the liquor store and bought a bottle of Dewar's White Label Blended Scotch Whisky. I left my car somewhere, I don't remember where (I think it was in New Jersey), and I went to a motel. I don't remember taking a taxi to get there but I must have. I do remember I took a taxi to get home, so I probably took one to get there. All night I drank, smoked cigarettes (Salem Premium Length that I carried in my big white tote bag big enough for a fifth, and six packs of cigarettes, and my make-up), and I had a yellow pad where all night I wrote down the heartaches of my life. (Later on I used that yellow pad to write down my life story for my sponsor, which sounds like almost the same thing, but there's a whole wide difference in attitude.) Note that this was—as I recall and reconstruct what happened—in the mixed-manic mode that—to me—distinguishes manic depression from "simple" bipolar illness.

Saturday (October 3rd) around noon I got a taxi home and I walked into the kitchen where my husband, two children (my two step-daughters, ages thirteen and four), and the dog were seated around the kitchen table having lunch. Well actually, the dog was sitting on the floor, but he looked at me the same way they did. No one asked me where I'd been or how I was—they just looked at me. They looked at me with a look I had come to recognize from my family when they didn't know what to do—they just looked at me. Naturally that Saturday night I drank, and then Sunday I drank again. My husband was supposed to leave town on a business trip Sunday, but he was afraid to leave me with the children, so he changed his plans and went to his office in Valley Forge. By the time he came home Monday evening I had once more begun drinking.

I had a few drinks and went into the kitchen to get another—it was early evening—and I found out there was no alcohol in the house! Now you understand I had always maintained an adequate supply in the house (some non-alcoholics might say more than adequate)—I might run out of ketchup but I wouldn't run out of Scotch—so I knew my husband must have poured it down the sink. I went into a rage—I was really out of my mind (I mean, even more than usually) at the thought I couldn't get a drink in my own house.

I called my husband horrible names and I took down two large carving knives off the kitchen knife rack and I went after him threatening to kill him—at the very least I wanted to hurt him a lot. (This is all definitely manic behavior.) He was a lot bigger than I was and he just flipped the knives out of my hands, and he laughed at me—which made me even more furious. I told him that when he went to bed, he better not close his eyes. And it could be some outside power intervened in my life that night (some people would call it God) because I not only didn't kill my husband, I didn't put a mark on him—I passed out pretty much peacefully in the living room before I could do anything more.

This is classic "irritable manic" or "angry manic" behavior (as well as drunken behavior), and it is one of the ways I have historically come out of depression (not in detail—no knives in other cases, at least in the years since I began the lithium therapy). And in this case, pre-lithium, my therapy was self-medication with alcohol. But I came out of the angry manic state (which had swiftly followed the depressed state) in a way familiar to me now from William James's *The Varieties of Religious Experience*—a book recommended for alcoholics in A. A. ever since Bill W. began reading it back in 1934. And there was something else now (2017 and before) familiar to me from William James and from Bill W., something about dreams.

DREAMING

For many years previous to 1970, at least ten, I had been a nightmare sleeper five or six nights a week. I had horrible dreams of rodents and reptiles and fences with spikes on them, and most nights I woke up screaming. This night however I didn't have a nightmare—I had what I now think of as my white dream. In the dream there was a large window with no curtains and glistering white sunlight poured in that window almost as white as diamonds. I had never had a dream like that before, and I just dismissed it—I didn't even mention it to my sponsor in A. A. (when I got a sponsor) for five or six months. I was glad the horrible nightmares had gone—they've never come back—but I really didn't think much about the dream itself.

What was the dream like? It's very hard to tell the story because the words I can find don't seem to describe what happened. But let me try. I saw the light, though I can't really describe its appearance (even "white" isn't quite right), and as soon as I saw it, it was like the design of things was opened to me. I sat there, all confused, and then my whole self that had been angry and "down" was suddenly "up"— like a switch from drowning to swimming. Experiences like mine are recorded in William James, *The Varieties of Religious Experience*—but why was my change with my white-light experience only (immediately) in my alcoholism (and so was Bill W's change, as the record tells us), while others apparently have been rescued all the way from manic depression?

I have thought about the possibility that the "white-light" experience actually represents a sudden shift in the paths of neurotransmission (trigger unknown), and I suppose that makes sense (the shift in neurotransmission accompanying John Newton's experience of "Amazing Grace" seems to have dealt with what I think was his alcoholism or at least his drinking alcoholically), but if someone was manic but didn't drink alcoholically, obviously he couldn't be changed away from alcoholic drinking. I could be, and was.

In any case—in my case—the day after the white-light dream was a totally different day from the days that had gone before. That morning—Tuesday—began differently from any day in a long time. I didn't drive to the liquor store; I didn't call the other liquor store that delivered to your home in an unmarked blue station wagon and even took a check; I didn't call my friend Kelly who lived four houses away and always had a good supply at her house. Instead I called the lady I had met the year before at the A. A. meeting. I asked her if they still had that meeting Tuesday night at the Episcopal Church there in Moorestown, and when she said they did, I told her I'd be there. I learned later she didn't think I would make it. But I did. By that first night after I had swallowed my last drink, I was at a meeting, had a sponsor, and had begun to try sobriety. We'll get to that "sponsor" business a little later on.

Why? Why the change in behavior? It's possible the timing of the apparent change from angry-manic to a kind of gentle fatigue, a change connected with a shattering or at least strong (neural / neuronal) effect of the dream, had something to do with it. So this step toward sobriety came at a kind of cusp between angry mania and a sudden shift toward an alternative state—but perhaps, through the dream, toward quiet (not manic but not depressed).

AFTER OCTOBER 5, 1970

Historically, in the years since 1970, October 5th has found me still "up" but not angry. By the end of the month, historically, I am down. For years I have given an A. A. talk as soon after my anniversary as I can: most of them have been toward the end of the month, when most Central Pennsylvania groups seem to have their Speaker's Meetings, and they haven't been very good, most of them—but when I spoke at a First Saturday meeting on October 5, 2013, it was among the very best talks I have given.

My first A. A. group urged service on me. In fact, this group in South Jersey wasn't sure that washing coffee cups and cleaning ashtrays was enough service for me, with my shaky sobriety (that was back when they had smoking meetings and no Styrofoam cups), so they created a new service position, Group Librarian. This was at a point, looking at my cycling, where I would have usually been in a bottom (I think), so the added responsibility was opportune. The last Tuesday of the month was the group's Anniversary Night, and the Group Librarian's responsibility was to keep track of the anniversaries.

So I kept track of anniversaries, and on Anniversary Night there would be a sheet-cake with everyone's name on it who had celebrated an anniversary that month. That was my beginning in service. I had to ask every member of the group when his or her sobriety date was (that member's "Date of Last Drink"). I was the member who came late, sat in the back of the room, didn't open my mouth, and didn't want to meet anyone. I had all these names down on pieces of paper and I stuffed them in my tote bag and I had a notebook—I didn't know what to do, list by anniversaries or list by members, so after some moments of panic, and calling my husband, I decided how to do it. In the first half of the book I listed anniversaries alphabetically by name and in the second half by anniversary month. It was a great book and served the purpose of getting me to talk to other members.

The big anniversary was the ninety-day anniversary. (For me this came on the way up from my bottom, but not yet to a "normal" level which doesn't actually exist: let's say an "average" level.) The ninety-day pins were very small gold pins in the shape of a triangle and at the top of the triangle was a pointed capital G. At the opposite corners of the triangle at each corner was an A. The top of the G made the point (apex) of the triangle. In the center of the triangle was a raised dot. There were no chips or medallions then in South Jersey, but ninety-day pins were presented in front of the group, by your sponsor, on the ninetieth day. The G was for God, the two As for A. A., and the dot is for you—as long as you stay between God and A. A. you will be well.

Then my sponsor asked if I'd made a decision about myself—after ninety days of sobriety, was I going to return to my previous life, or was I going to stay with sobriety? I and everyone else I ever heard said we were going to stay with sobriety. I don't know if pins like that are still used, but I still have mine. It was a small unassuming pin— actually a stud you could put into a button hole. The ninety-day pin was not sponsored by A. A., but just like the chips and medallions today, was provided by an independent provider. (Like the job as Librarian, this involved my making a public commitment, to bring myself out of myself.)

The moment my sponsor asked me what my decision was, I actually didn't know. I couldn't think that far ahead for anything that important, but I was terrified to say that. I was afraid everyone would think me a dummy, so I said I was going to continue on this path. It was like being sworn into a secret society, or being accepted as a candidate for knighthood, or something like that. I was trembling and red with blushing and nervousness and really frightened when I sat down, and told myself I was going to take the Scarlett O'Hara approach, and think about all that tomorrow. But my answer to my sponsor was prophetic. I'm still a member of that society now, forty-seven years later.

Looking back on my pre-Lithium days in Alcoholics Anonymous, on making amends for my past actions, I realize the behavior I needed to make amends for must have been pretty uniformly behavior in a manic phase. What I'm not sure of is what good behavior might also have come in a manic state. One case I remember very clearly—with an impact on me not unlike the white-light dream, in my pre-lithium A. A. life, came from my going to the Camden County Jail (Women's) back in 1970-71. One of my first reactions to the Camden County [Women's] Jail back then was being happy that, when we finished our meeting, the door closed and locked with Kathy and me on the right side of it.

You might say, that was a true feeling, and it has remained with me. But that was only the very beginning. If you go into A. A., you'll find that not all service opportunities have or will have the shattering and life-revising effect that Camden County Jail had on me—and forty-six-plus years later, I'm not sure this part of my story has stopped developing yet. I can see more clearly now, partly because I can think more clearly now, because my mind has learned new ways of thinking—in fact, my brain has learned new patterns of neural transmission—through year after year of sobriety. That was one of the things the Jail did—and the dream did.

Some months after I got to A. A.—but before I was on lithium—I met a very exciting man who invited me to dinner. We had dinner in New Hope and he invited me to go to the Holiday Inn. I had my own car—a dark-green Pontiac convertible—which was very recognizable and I parked it out front next to his.

We were in the room. I took off my dress and was preparing to take off my slip—gals wore slips in those days—when there was a huge crash and the door to the room came right down on the floor. Standing there were my husband and my brother. I was terrified and I think my date was too. He wasn't the biggest guy in the world and my brother and husband were big. My brother went over and talked to my date—I think maybe to assure him they weren't going to kill him. My husband saw that I put my clothes on. And my brother took the keys to my car. We left for home. As I said, I was terrified.

At this time, we'd sold the house we built, and we lived in a big apartment building in Valley Forge and in the elevator my husband took my clothes off and... When we got home to the apartment he took my clothes off again and threw me on the bed and I was ravaged. Of course I didn't know then but I learned later on that the date at the Holiday Inn was part of my high manic cycle.

When I was young, long before A. A., even before I took my first drink, there used to be a game called "Whisper Down the Lane"— I've heard people in other places called it "Telephone"—where you would whisper something to the person next to you, and they would whisper it to the person next to them, and so on down the line, until it got to the person who started it, and then everyone would laugh at how the message got all messed up. But this is "Whisper Down the

Lane" in reverse. Every time I hear myself tell my story; every time I hear you tell your story; every time I hear a speaker or read a story in the back of the Big Book or even listen to a tape; I hear it better and better, and I see the true pattern better and better.

But formal instruction may be necessary when we are in some ways estranged and yet in a position (or a colleague is in a position) of having been in some way a victim of whispering—particularly to oneself. That also resets the course of neurons in their transmission through the brain—but not favorably. (And I know that my recovery from alcoholism—my life's goal and work—has aided in my living my bipolar life. I don't know if any particular goal, rigorously sought, would do this: but this is what happened with me.)

ADULTHOOD: DR. ZARATE, LITHIUM, SOBRIETY, MARRYING/NOT MARRYING

Several months after the Holiday Inn episode I went into a real downswing. It was a 4th of July celebration at my mother's and on the 3rd of July I went into my mother's kitchen and took off all my clothes. She called my husband and told him to get me out of there.

My husband had met a doctor named Carlos A. Zarate. He called the doctor and the doctor said, "Get her into the hospital" and I wouldn't go. So the doctor said "Take a bathrobe and put it on her backwards and it will function as a straightjacket." So my husband got my brother and the straightjacket and my brother held me in the back of the car while my husband drove me to the hospital. This was at about 11 at night. They took me in and tried to calm me down and sit me in a chair and I was extremely uncooperative. They kept me in the straightjacket and put me in a bed and I couldn't move. They wanted to give me an injection to calm me down but they didn't know what I had had before coming to the hospital, so they didn't know what to give me to calm me down, so they didn't give me an injection.

They thought maybe, if they could feed me they might make a little progress, but I wouldn't let them feed me anything. I insisted everything had ground glass in it. They got so fed up with me that they put me in a side room in a Posey—a Posey is a belt that straps you in, so there I was in a side room, strapped into a bed with no lights, no clothes but like a nightgown shift, and I couldn't get up to go to the bathroom. Naturally I kept wetting my pants, and of course when you wet your pants they get very cold and damp and it's very uncomfortable. When I finally came to, in this side room by myself, in bed with a Posey strap, I did not know who I was and where I was, I was catatonic. I had to be fed, and at first the only thing I would eat was yogurt. I had decided yogurt didn't have ground glass in it.

The bed I was strapped in was in the middle of the room, so I couldn't touch the walls, but I had these hallucinations I mentioned in the vignette at the beginning, that my head was disconnected from my body and bouncing around and hitting things. The window was barred and the door of the room was barred, and from my bed I couldn't see anything outside the room. But I found out later that there was sometimes a volleyball game going on outside, and I think I heard the volleyball bouncing, and being served or hit during the game, and the sound of the ball bouncing was what translated to my head bouncing around the room.

They finally took me once in a while to the bathroom and to say the least I thought they were really nasty. Of course, on their behalf, I should say—and I do say, now—that they were dealing with a very difficult patient and a very sick one. I was in the side room for about a week and a half and then they decided to let me out. I was in a regular room, but I was notified that, if I didn't behave myself I would go back into the side room.

After a few days I was allowed to wear real clothes and my meals were upstairs. Eventually I was allowed down the huge staircase to the dining room and after all I'd been through the dining room was like a palace and I could eat anything I wanted and even have seconds.

Then they began to introduce the lithium carbonate and I did not do well. I had tremendous tremors and it was nothing for me to take a spoonful of cereal and the tremor would be so great the cereal wound up thrown across the room.

I can still see that and the table I was sitting at. Then one day the nurse came up to me with a little plate of crackers covered with peanut butter. There were about half a dozen crackers on the plate— no, maybe four or five. I asked what they were for and I was told just to eat the crackers: the doctor had ordered them. After a week or two my tremors were gone and with just a few minor exceptions they have not returned. That was a little more than forty years ago.

No, I don't think the peanut butter had a physical therapeutic effect itself—unless somehow the peanut butter reduced the tremors not only psychologically (it's a "comfort food") but physiologically—but I do think it must have been necessary to get the lithium into me rather than jerked onto the wall or the floor. It's a good thing I loved peanut butter (And I still do). But let me tell you a little about Carlos A. Zarate.

He was an Argentinian who played [I think competitive] amateur tennis, and who had studied in Europe, where lithium carbonate had been used before it had been approved (or re-approved) in the United States in late 1970. I believe it is his son, Carlos, Jr., who is now head of the Mood Disorders section at NIMH and a clinical professor at George Washington. It must run in the blood. I hated Dr. Zarate at the start.

That hospital was an expensive place, fine linen and all that. We had waiters in the dining-room (I was finally allowed to go there) and the patients were allowed to request second helpings. There was one nice nurse—I later found out she was a stone alcoholic—but the rest were not nice. (This, by the way, was the second fancy hospital I'd been in—the first was Dufour, back before Norristown, well before sobriety, back in the days around my first marriage.

That was where I had the shock treatments, where I finally didn't know who I was and where I was and who anyone else was—including my mother. Dufour was across the road from what had been my grandfather's house, and after I was "well" enough to walk outside—accompanied—I kept thinking that house looked familiar. But I couldn't figure out it had been my grandfather's.

It was on October 5th, 1972, that I told Dr. Zarate I needed to go home. It was my A. A. anniversary and I wanted to get to a meeting and I had been there at the hospital since the 3rd of July. So he let me go home, and he said I would have to come back if I acted up. I never acted up that way again.

Remember that it was Dr. Zarate who said my treatment for manic depression was lithium and my treatment for alcoholism was A. A. and I had to keep both of them up. And from here on, the story of my bipolar life is the story of my bipolar life in recovery from alcoholism. My goal could have been success in business, or in politics, or even in having a large family. But it wasn't: it was and is recovery.

AFTER OCTOBER 5, 1970

After October 5ᵗʰ, 1972, I was on both lithium and A. A., and while the timing of the cyclothymic patterns, even the change-dates, remained similar, the cycles were somewhat flattened out, but so long as I was at Dr. Zarate's prescribed lithium level, and was in familiar (Philadelphia-based) surroundings, with a good A. A. sponsor and other strong members around me, things seemed to be going well—and I think they were. When my son was born in 1979, I had to restrict my A. A. service geographically—but it was still in and around Philadelphia and with familiar people.

Then, in February 1988, after my mother's death (in 1987), my (third) husband, Vince, took a job in Central Pennsylvania. I found a new version of A. A., new medical advisors, needed a new Sponsor, and things were not as good as they had been. Vince adjusted to the A. A. in Central Pennsylvania better than I did, though I did find a pretty good sponsor locally. But there were some signs of trouble even before that. I mention this next situation here because it's relevant (I think) to the interconnection of my alcoholism and my manic depression.

The Philadelphia A. A. old-timers really didn't miss much: I can remember lingering in the parking lot after a meeting talking to a man, and someone coming up to me and saying, "Isn't it time for you to get home?" I was wild, and I thought, who are they to be saying that?—but after that I never lingered in a parking lot after a meeting talking to a man.

There was another old-timer a little later—actually Rita wasn't really an old timer but she had that aura—she came up to me after a meeting—she was a little gal with tiny fingers and I can still see her little finger poking at my chest when she said, "You, my dear, are not getting to enough meetings!"

I was so wild I didn't go to that meeting for a while and I didn't speak to Rita or her husband even if I saw them at other meetings or around —I had a terrible resentment though I didn't know that's what it was—she wasn't even my sponsor and she spoke to me like that! After about a month I had to say something about it to someone. It was festering inside me. My brother picked me up for a meeting and I told him about it and asked him what he thought.

He said Rita was right—this from my own brother—and I thought the God I was now believing in had turned on me. He not only said Rita was right, he said that the minute it happened I should have spoken to someone about it. I said sarcastically, "Well, who exactly do you think I should have talked to about it?" and he said, "Anyone, sister—it didn't matter just so long as you got rid of that burden." It took me quite a while to get over all this—what Rita said and what my brother said— but I did, and in the end I got to see that Rita was right—I wasn't getting to enough meetings. I stepped up my meeting attendance: then I was able to say to Rita, "You remember that night you said I wasn't getting to enough meetings—you were right."

When I came home from the hospital and was on my lithium, and I was sober, I thought everything would be all right. I loved my husband; he loved me; he got along fantastically well with my mother. He had introduced me to his parents up in Shenandoah (Pennsylvania), and I think I was one of his father's favorite people. His father was diabetic, and after a life in the coal mines he rented some farmland and raised and canned (or bottled or "jarred") fruits and vegetables suitable for diabetics, and won awards for them.

And you can imagine how much my mother appreciated the plumbing and electrical and carpentry abilities my husband had learned in night school. But it wasn't just that—when she was still drinking, after I was sober, she fell and broke her ankle, and it was my husband (we were still married then) who took her to the hospital, and told her, "Kay, you have to stop this drinking"—and he was the only one who could talk to her about it that she would talk with. My first three husbands got along very well with my mother— my present husband, of course, didn't get to know her at all—except from my memories.

NOT MARRYING ANDREW'S FATHER

It was at this point, when I was sober five or six years, I developed thyroid cancer—I was treated twice with liquid radiation and I was afraid and my family was very afraid—my mother especially. I was having some trouble with dizziness and brief faints at a time I was very active in A. A., on the steering committee of a large city intergroup, and I went to my doctor for a checkup and told him I was worried about driving my car, and should I cut back on my activities—since I had this medical problem maybe I was into too much and maybe I should drop some things. He said to me "Miss S____ don't you drop anything, you stay as close to this A. A. as you can—if you need to."

My second husband and I had been divorced about a year—maybe two—when I was diagnosed with a thyroid malignancy. I was given radioactive treatment and it was supposed to be finished in one treatment—and it wasn't. So I had to stop taking my lithium for a brief time (the only time I was ever off) and stop taking my birth-control pills so they could do a second treatment, which took. Meanwhile I replaced the birth-control pills with vaginal foam. And one evening I used the foam once but made love twice—and then shortly realized I was pregnant. The man in my life had told me he was a confirmed bachelor.

That didn't bother me at all till I became pregnant—and so help me I thought in that case we would get married. He reminded me that he was a confirmed bachelor, and then let me know—besides that—he wouldn't marry me even if he were the marrying kind because I was crazy. But I was going to have that baby. When I found out I was pregnant I told my mother and she had begged me not to go the abortion route. I told her I had no intention of going that route. I thought of this baby as coming straight from heaven. She was delighted and months before Andrew was born she started sending him little welcome cards, saying that she loved him and she couldn't wait to see him. She was in the waiting room when he was born.

ANDREW'S BIRTH AND EARLY LIFE

I was upset by the absence of marriage but at the same time I was thrilled that I was having a child. I was thirty-seven when the child was conceived; thirty-eight when he was born. I had a very fine obstetrician and followed all the directions he gave me, from exercise to diet to—well, everything else. I ate good healthy regular meals and I exercised every single day. I didn't like the exercising but I did it. I had no sickness, no dizziness. I felt like a million bucks and I had a very easy delivery with a friend of mine as my delivery coach. My brother had married by that time, a divorcee with two children. She had volunteered to be my coach, and then she changed her mind.

Angie then picked herself as my coach because, she said, with her lifestyle (she was lesbian) she would never have a baby or see one born and she wanted to be there to help me when this baby was born. And she was a wonderful coach.

I nursed my son and I did exercises again after the delivery and I felt really good. I had some money so I didn't work for the first year of Andrew's life (well, almost). We traveled. I took him all sorts of places. When he was eleven months old I put him in a very fine daycare and I went to work. Putting him in daycare was the hardest thing I've ever done. The second day at daycare when I brought him home he started to throw up—projectile vomiting—in the car and it continued while I drove him home. I was very afraid for him and I called a very good friend of mine who was a Christian Scientist and she prayed for Andrew and she told me to pray for him—I did—we both prayed for him and he stopped vomiting immediately. He never started up again.

Andrew was a healthy child (except for that brief projectile vomiting). He didn't have chickenpox or any of those things, but did break his collarbone when he was about eighteen months old. I never knew how he did it, maybe falling out of the crib (or trying to get out). He cried and cried and I didn't know what was wrong. I took him to our family doctor and he sent him to the hospital for x-rays and he did have a broken collar bone. The people at the hospital didn't know how he got it—he was so small—and the other thing was, he had stopped crying. They put a brace on him and he healed quickly and all was well.

The other injury he had was a broken finger. That healed quickly. He didn't get real bad sick colds or the flu. His eating habits were strange for a while: he would only eat only one thing for days at a time—"Spaghettio's" breakfast lunch and dinner—or hot dogs—or mac and cheese. Another repeat food was an 'omlid' (that's an omelette, very often a "cheese omlid") three times a day for several weeks—and then switch.

He was a big milk drinker—sometimes Kool-Aid. (Maybe this isn't actually strange—maybe many children do it—but it was strange to me, and when I was down it worried me greatly, and when I was up I thought it was humorous—even really funny. It seems funny now.)

His behavior in daycare was often a little wild—and that contin-ued into kindergarten, 1st grade, 2nd grade—and all the rest of his school. School behavior was never really good. Of course he doesn't remember what was going through his mind in those days, but I wonder if it was not having a father or having a bi-polar mother or both that made him that way. There's no way I'll ever be able to know for sure, in this life. Anyhow, by his second grade, I had married my third husband (Andrew was five), or maybe Andrew and I had married my third husband.

In the years afterwards, Andrew didn't graduate from high school because he couldn't stand to go to school any longer. When he was at the halfway house (that story comes a little later, with the tale of the eighteen bongs), he got his GED—doing well on the tests. One thing happened that was particularly important for Andrew, and I've already mentioned it—when he was five. I married my third husband, and Andrew had a wonderful stepfather. And all along, till he was seven and a half, he had a wonderful grandmother—mostly. My mother never remarried after my father's death and the greatest joy of her life after he was born was her grandson. (The last Christmas in her life, when Andrew was seven, every present she bought was for him—my brother wasn't happy. I think he counted everything she bought for her grandson as a present for me—it certainly wasn't a present for him.)

Before his (first) stepfather came along, Andrew's father saw him maybe at most a couple of times a year. I don't know who it was, who was the main male influence in Andrew's life, but one of the influences was my Uncle Mike, who taught him how to swear and how to spit—in the toilet, not on the floor, as he pointed out to me when I spoke to him about it. "Well, Geranium (what my Uncle Mike called me), would you rather I told him to spit on the floor?"

The swearing was mostly the f-word and that didn't go down well at the Little People Day Care after Andrew had spent one weekend with Uncle Mike. "He just goes around saying the f-word over and over again, Mrs. S------." I think that was when he left that daycare, though it might have been shortly after that—there were so many daycares and nursery schools and my memory still hasn't, after all these years, completely recovered from the ECT.

THIRD MARRIAGE—A STEPFATHER FOR ANDREW

The re-gathering of my family itself apparently minimized the effects of my manic depression. At least, I believe my mental balance was better between 1974 (my mother got sober) and 1987 (my mother died) than before or possibly (but not certainly) since. Now one of the characteristics of manic depression, as I have been taught, is that it comes and goes more or less regularly without triggers. But, from my experience, its depth can be triggered, or something like it. It seems like, if I'm on the way down, and something bad happens, I may go further down than I would otherwise. On the other hand, if my circumstances are more than usually pleasant, my down may be less down than usual. The year after my mother died, my husband got a new job, and we moved to Central Pennsylvania, away from Uncle Mike, and my brother had moved to Minnesota (with his new wife), and A. A. in Central Pennsylvania was not like A. A. in the Philadelphia area. And my next downturn was further down, and the upturn not so far up.

But I still had my son Andrew, when and he was with us as we searched for a house in Central Pennsylvania, in Elizabethtown, suddenly he and my husband picked the house they said we had to buy—in the dark of night with little light to see it by. Andrew was fascinated by the den closet with access to the attic (it was a one-story house)—many years later he told me seeing that closet was (he was eight years old) his first dateable memory. He was excited and happy, and that must have affected me. I got a new sponsor, in the adjacent town of Mt. Joy, whom I liked and appreciated (and sometimes fought with). And people in Lancaster County were just plain different from people in and around Philadelphia,

All this brings up—in retrospect—a possibility I hadn't thought much about before It almost looks like a "good" period could be triggered by a "good" event—but we know, don't we, that the ups and downs of manic depression aren't triggered? True, but suppose it's the good state that triggers the good event (not all good events, of course, but at the least, if I'm "up," I'm more likely to treat an event as "good"—as an opportunity, rather than a problem, something to be avoided or short-circuited rather than an opportunity to be grasped). We'll come back to that.

My third husband's love for Andrew was deep and reciprocated. They were a great combination. Andrew and his stepfather were going out and I said, "Don't let him have a whole lot of chocolate," because they had told me at his nursery school that he shouldn't have much chocolate. They came home and Andrew had a lot of chocolate on his face. I said to Andrew "Where did you get the chocolate?" He looked at me with those big eyes and said, "In a truck."

My husband took Andrew every Friday afternoon to go shopping at Toys 'R Us, and Andrew was allowed to pick out anything he wanted And he did, and he had a room full of wonderful things. They also went out for lunch every Saturday—to a place called the Blue Willow. Lunch was usually hot roast beef sandwiches with gravy and mashed potatoes and a coke float. My third husband was an orphan who was severely wounded in Korea and could not have children.

When he met Andrew it was a little like love at first sight. I think I got married this time because it was a life for Andrew—and the two of them got along fantastically well with each other. And Vincent understood boys—and certainly Andrew—far better than I did then, or apparently ever could. Sometimes I was truly happy with this; sometimes I felt left out.

When Andrew got into a fight with a playmate who had a toy gun, and he took the gun away from him, my husband told me, "Jane, Andrew is a boy and he is going to have a desire for a gun and if you don't let him have one he is going to get one any way he can." Andrew returned the gun to the boy and he and his stepfather went out shopping, and Andrew got his gun, and there was never another such problem. Interestingly, Andrew is now thirty-eight years old (or almost), and not so much interested in guns. He has the antique gun that was my father's, but he does not now use it (it may be unusable) or any other gun.

When Andrew was born in 1979, I had to restrict my A. A. service geographically—but it was still in and around Philadelphia, and with familiar people. Then, in February 1988, after my mother's death (in March 1987), my (third) husband, Vince, took a job in Central Pennsylvania. I found a new version of A. A. and had to get a new sponsor, and things were not as good as they had been. Vince adjusted to the A. A. in Central Pennsylvania better than I did, though I did find a pretty good sponsor. And even before the move, there were some signs of trouble in my life, from bipolar complications, I believe. I can remember lingering in the parking lot after a meeting, talking to a man, and someone coming up to me and saying, "Isn't it time for you to get home?" I was wild, and I thought, who are they to be saying that?—but after that I never lingered in a parking lot, after a meeting, talking to a man.

Over the years, one of the most difficult parts (for me) of the process of recovery from alcoholism has been A. A.'s Step Ten ("Continued to take personal inventory, and when we were wrong, promptly admitted it"). It's been hard for me to evaluate what I've done; when I'm "down," it seems very bad and when I'm "up," it doesn't really seem bad at all. It took me till after I had done Step Eleven ("Sought through prayer and meditation to improve our conscious contact with God....") and Step Twelve ("Having had a spiritual awakening as the result of these Steps, we tried to carry this message to alcoholics, and to practice these principles in all our affairs") to begin to be able to do Step Ten. What happened is that, being unable to rely on my mind to examine and classify my misdeeds, I found myself able to rely on my gut reactions. When I was doing my "spot-check" inventory before praying at night, even if it was a day when I got along and everything seemed to be going well, everything was fine, God in his heaven and all's well with the world, somehow I began to feel a little bit uncomfortable, a little bit queasy.

There's an old saying that your head can lie to you six days out of seven, but your gut will never lie to you. I don't know if that's true, but I get this queasy feeling and I know something is wrong— something I've said, something I've done, some attitude that has crept in. For example, I've been known to be sarcastic and think nothing of it, but others don't "think nothing of it," and I need to make a spot-check inventory on my sarcasm and do something about it, and do something about the damage it's done.

If my grandson is getting on my nerves (he's twenty-two and lives with us, and he does get on my nerves sometimes), and if I reprove him or complain, I lose contact with him that I need for both our sakes (and my husband's, who, after all, also lives here), and then I have to repair and correct what I've done—no matter how reasonable it seemed at the time. (Funny thing, I think of Andrew and Jeffrey, both of whom grew up in this house, as my boys—though they are father and son, and very different from each other—quite apart from the eight inches by which Jeffrey is taller than his father.)

I'm thinking—and I can tell you all (my book-readers) and tell every alcoholic I've ever sponsored—we need to know how our harsh words can hurt, and that hurt can go on and on, if we don't make our spot-check inventory and do something about the hurting we have caused. Sometimes, when I'm shifting from up to down or down to up, I'll do the spot-check inventory and know I have to correct the situation—and then it gets away from me in the shift.

It's like sometimes the task is twice as hard, and even after forty-seven years, I don't do as well as I should, or haven't done as well as I should have. My guess is that this would apply regardless of what life goal I was working for. Of course, for me, as for many "bipolars" who are also alcoholic, one major goal is sobriety.

To get back to my narrative, it was when Andrew was twelve that my third husband died of lung cancer. I have never thought that made any sense—now when he particularly needed him Andrew didn't have a stepfather—and he still didn't see his real father. I remember about his hitting the kid and taking his gun—I didn't like my son having a gun, but I had faith in what my husband told me. He was the kind of person you always believed. You just knew that what he was telling you was real and true. He was always that way—and that must have been what that little boy saw in him.

As I said, Vincent died when Andrew was twelve, of lung cancer, at the age of sixty-one, four years after we had moved—because of his new job—from the Philadelphia area to Central Pennsylvania, to the Susquehanna Valley, where I live now. We moved the year after my mother died.

I should perhaps repeat for emphasis that, like my second husband, my third husband was very fond of my mother, very much at her service. (In fact, when my second husband—second ex-husband by then—was helping her with the electrical work and plumbing and carpentry at her second Blue Skies, my third husband was working on the pond and the drainage. That was the pond my son Andrew fell in and Mother's dog dragged him out.) Of course, my third husband had known my mother before we were married, and being himself independent and Irish, perhaps he admired those qualities in her. In any case, they got along very well indeed. But then she and my second husband got along, and he was Polish, from the coalfields of Shenandoah, Pennsylvania—and my mother was *not* Polish. Nor did she have the reputation of being particularly easy to get along with.

AFTER A SECOND DEATH FROM LUNG CANCER

When Andrew was twelve, right after my third husband's death, he got into trouble at the Donegal Middle School, with a teacher who claimed he struck her (after she attacked him, in my view). She was implacable and determined to revenge herself on this unruly twelve-year-old. If my husband had been alive, he could have stood up to her, and would have made sure things worked out right. As it was, Andrew was scheduled for the Barnes Hall juvenile facility, and I didn't know what to do. I talked to one of my Christian Science friends who suggested we send Andrew to boarding school. Dottie and I made a list, looked around, and found that his record in school pretty much precluded his acceptance.

I approached—I think—eighteen schools, and the only one which would take him was Valley Forge Military Academy, and they took him—but I had to raise $25000—which I did, by taking a loan on my car and taking a loan from a local bank—I couldn't take a loan on the house because it was still under partial foreclosure. When I took him out to school the first day I was short, and I wasn't sure they would take him, but they said "Mrs. S----- we will take him but you'll have to get the money to us as soon as you can." He got 420 demerits and he was out before I got the rest of the money to them. But he was there at Valley Forge Military Academy when his case came up in juvenile court, and I told the judge he had been enrolled at Valley Forge Military Academy, which made the case moot as far as the Donegal School was concerned. I eventually paid off the car loan and finally renegotiated my mortgage.

Was this a rational decision? A panic decision?

One interview question for Andrew at Valley Forge Military Academy—what was the worst thing you've ever done? (I wasn't there for this question or the answer). It turned out he was a piker measured against some of the other kids. One of the greatest things about that school I remember was the military tattoo, around Thanksgiving time, and all the students were there and all the parents, and they had marching bands and music and one of the songs was "Amazing Grace." I don't think there was a dry eye in the house.

I thought Valley Forge Military Academy would straighten Andrew out, and they did, more or less, for eight or nine months, until my money ran out—and Andrew accumulated a record number of demerits. So he came home again, this time to the local high school, which he sometimes attended, occasionally enjoyed, and did little work for. When he went back to public school, he hated it.

"Mother I just can't stand it," He dropped out of public school at sixteen—or technically finally dropped out when he was seventeen. He did work for a while at K-Mart or Radio-Shack or one or another of those places in the little strip mall in the town (I think it was both K-Mart and Radio-Shack). Before that, when he was about fourteen or fifteen, a couple of years after his stepfather's death, I got a phone call from his father, saying he wanted to see me. His father had paid child support and he had seen Andrew maybe half a dozen times. When he came to see me he said he wanted to make amends to me for the way he treated me when I was pregnant—he wouldn't marry me; he wouldn't come to see me; he wouldn't come to see the baby.

About six months after he came to see me he died. I got a phone call from his sister. It was a very small funeral. His will left an annuity to Andrew and me and everything else—not a great deal—to Andrew. This was a surprise to me, and it did soften my feelings towards him. I had been very bitter and angry. I don't know if I was angry-manic.

A couple of years before, in 1992, when my third husband died of lung cancer, a good friend of mine suggested I go to college. I thought I would never be able to do that. I had not finished high school—far from it—though I had gotten a GED (in New Jersey) when I was thirty and newly sober.

My friend drove me to HACC [Harrisburg Area Community College] in Harrisburg, twenty miles up the road. I was terrified but I followed the instructions I was given, and I took the test for admission and placement.

Then someone gave me a list of courses to take. I right away saw Criminal Justice and I thought that was the one for me. I was fifty-two years old and she didn't think that was appropriate. She suggested I try Art History. I insisted on Criminal Justice, and I loved it and I did extremely well. (When I took an Art History course I did very well on that, too, but CJ was what I wanted. It all went back to that morning at the Camden County Jail (Women's).

My brother had been divorced out in Minnesota and came to live with me two months after my third husband's death. He would leave every few months and Andrew would help him pack up—then he'd come back. The last time he didn't come back but died at a friend's house. My brother and son got along better than my brother and I did.

At the end of my course at HACC there was a banquet for Honors students and we were allowed to bring a guest. I took my brother. The dinner was fair; there were a couple of speakers; we were on our way home and Teddy said to me, "I never thought I'd say this but I'm proud of you for doing this. You're really smarter than I thought". This was the only time I remember his paying me a compliment—and I will remember that ride home forever. I'm remembering it now with tears. My son was totally proud of me as were my friends and I was amazed.

LATER ADULTHOOD: THIS MARRIAGE AND THE LAST TWENTY-TWO YEARS

I was writing this with my husband—actually I'm dictating it to him—just as I did with my first book, when he asked me, "Aren't you leaving something out?" I asked him what it was he had in mind, and he said, "Well, you've been undergoing lithium therapy for more than forty years—forty-four now [it's now forty-five]—and for more than forty percent of that time you've been married to me. I don't mean that I'm particularly important here, but you really don't have much on the years since our marriage, except Andrew's problems and the doctors monkeying around with your lithium."

You know, it's easy to think of twenty years of living here in Elizabethtown (with my husband and our dogs—one at a time—and cats) as the present, except that our second dog had to be put down while we were writing this, and that's one mark between present and past. But I still feel his presence in the house. My husband takes the trash—garbage and recycle—out to the curb every Wednesday morning at 5 a.m.; he commuted to work every weekday; until just over a year ago when his position was revised out of existence; we go to A. A. meetings up to six nights a week. There's not a lot of variation. Our grandson grows a year older every year; we got a new car in 2000 and that was traded in and we got a new car in 2011, and we traded it in and got a new smaller car this year (2016); we've gone to different churches over the years—and, most important, I had an attack of CNS (central nervous system) vasculitis [giant-cell arteritis] in 2002, costing me most of my eyesight and forcing my disability retirement from the state.

Then the local community college where he was teaching decided to go for younger teachers, and played around with it just enough to make a suit for age discrimination difficult. But then he got a job with a local state agency in Harrisburg. (But his job was trying to help people whose student loans were fouled up, and a year ago the agency decided those problems should just be treated as "consumer complaints"—no action! Now he's out of a job again. But it's giving him time to work with me on this—and then to finish off some of his *long* term projects.)

It was a couple of years after my (third) husband died (I remember it as being longer), I realized my son was playing with drugs and my brother had come to live with me after his divorce and he had been diagnosed with lung cancer. I was at a low point in my life (and I may have been on a "down" though I'm not sure) and I went into a meeting one Wednesday night in tears. I looked across the table and there was a man I had never seen before. Sometime during the meeting I asked if there was anyone who could take my son to NA meetings, anyone who went to NA and AA.

After the meeting the man who had been sitting across from me came and introduced himself and said he could take my son to an NA meeting he went to. About a month later my son called him, and he began taking him to the NA meeting he went to, which was Monday night in Carlisle, across the river from where we lived. About two months later I invited him to the house for Sunday chicken—and about two years after that we were married.

My son gave me away, and the invitations were sent out in his name. Our early marriage was not an easy time. First off, my son was notified by the court to appear for DNA testing concerning the birth of a little boy a couple of years before—and the DNA showed that my son was indeed the father, and I found myself an unexpected grandmother of a little boy, two years old and a few months, whom I hadn't yet seen.

Not long after—Andrew was eighteen—I came home from the store (my husband was setting up for a meeting) and there was a whole gang—twelve or thirteen of Andrew's "friends"—using drugs in my house. I called the police and said I wanted them out of my house, and they were out of my house. The next thing I noticed the policeman and another policeman were carrying what looked like bottles out of the house and putting them in two police cars. I asked them what they were and they said "Ma'am, these are bongs." I had never heard of bongs, and he straightened me out as to what they were for, and Andrew was not allowed in the house again. (My husband just reminded me that I went with him to a meeting that night, then excused myself to go home before the meeting started, and then called the police, because I was afraid my husband wouldn't approve of my calling them.)

After he was nearly two weeks on the street, Andrew and the County made the decision for him to go to an alcohol and drug rehab. He went to the rehab outside Philadelphia for the full thirty days (no, I guess it was twenty-eight, because he got out on the same date in March that he went in there in February). Then he went to the halfway house up in Lewisburg, quite a distance away. Their transportation system failed and so my husband and I drove Andrew from the rehab to the halfway house, making sure he didn't get out of the car on the way, because we didn't legally have custody of him for the trip.

He spent part of his time drawing "Get me out of here" on the back window in the moisture there—you could see it when the car heated up for years afterward. It isn't still there—though it would be interesting to see if there might be any signs of it left (we still have the car, our 1995 Escort). Andrew was driving that car for a couple of years—it now has more than a quarter of a million miles on it— then Jeffrey, Andrew's son, now twenty-two, had a car (he works at a Ford agency), but used the old car as a winter-weather backup..

So we took Andrew to the halfway house, and we came up to visit him pretty often—more than any other parents ever had visited anyone there. We brought up our dog Pinky (for Pink Floyd— Andrew had named her) and we brought up Jeffrey a couple of times—when we asked the people at the house if we could bring up Andrew's son, they asked, "What son?" He hadn't told them about Jeffrey. We brought Jeffrey up the night we went to the A. A. meeting where Andrew got his nine-month sobriety chip—and the first picture we have of them together shows Andrew carrying Jeffrey on his shoulder, across the street, in front of the meeting place. You can see, to me, this was a high point. Once again, I don't know if it was a high point just because of how I felt, possibly being on the high part of an upswing in mood, or because in some objective way it really was a high point—and, as in other ups and downs, whether the two are so mixed together that there's no way to tell the difference— if there is one.

After the halfway house Andrew stayed up there for another couple of months in a "three-quarter" house run by a halfway-house alumnus who was a dedicated collector of Native American arti- facts—including many from the Conoy tribe living in the area where we live, who are in Jeffrey's ancestry on his mother's mother's side.

Somehow Andrew couldn't get a job there, near the three-quarter house, but he could get one in our town, where his then-current girl- friend was. Even though he was up there and the job was down here. When he went to K-mart after the halfway house (and the "three- quarter" house) he told them he had stolen things there before but they gave him the job anyway. He's a very good worker and (I believe) already something of a super-salesman. And that brings up something else, from the trips up to see Andrew, on the way up to Lewisburg, on Route 15, there was a place, along the river, where I could feel the Native American presence. Imagination? Telepathy? Senses at a high point? I don't know.

Andrew went to meetings for several years (and a girlfriend or two) afterwards, and then he stopped. I'm hopeful he's still sober;: in ny case, he's growing up, living with his current girlfriend and her little daughter in Lancaster, and looking more and more like my father. Jeffrey, on the other hand, looks more like my mother's brothers and my brother Ted. He's six inches taller than his father. But they get along together well.

The story of the bongs doesn't end with their seizure. Several years later my husband and I were away for the weekend: when we came home, our house had been robbed. We called the police. I asked the detective who came by—who had been at the house the night of the bongs—whatever happened to those eighteen bongs you took out of here? He laughed and he said "We had them on display for police from five or six jurisdictions so they'd know what was going on in this area. I guess in a way your son was famous."

My husband (that is, my fourth and present husband) is technically Andrew's stepfather, but Andrew is thirty-eight, and in any case, his "real" stepfather was my third husband. That's the one he had that relationship with. My husband is pretty much Jeffrey's grandfather (though that's actually a "step" relationship too), but they seem over the years to have come to some kind of a mutually acceptable relationship. In fact, the story of our twenty years of marriage is in a fairly large part the story of Jeffrey in our household: he now lives with us full-time (though I'm beginning to think he's going to move out and move in with his girlfriend in the not-very-distant future— but my husband says he can't afford it, and of course my feelings and belief here fluctuate, or, I should say, cycle). On average Jeffrey has lived with us half-time or more over his life since we found out he was our grandson.

All the memorable events I've described here come before or after 'plain' situations—life isn't an unending series of stealing boats and Holiday Inns or academic Honors Dinners or Mustang convertibles and all that—or even bongs in the bedroom. Some of the rest of life is—or seems—calm or maybe even "normal" or depressed. And going along in the quiet times you feel like you might be a normal person living a normal life—and the next thing you know there's another episode—a hospitalization, a manic spree, or a desire to die, and life is one of these damned things after another. Even the routine isn't always routine.

Every year I start out setting up a new organization—folders and all for files—for the year's papers, bills paid, bills to pay, car, insurance, mortgage, water, electric, or whatever—and every year, part way through, I can't find the bills, the car registrations, the insurance certificates. I get the month's bills together and some of them are current and some of them definitely are not. I have to get my husband to help me straighten them out.

He claims one problem is that when I'm cleaning things up, I occasionally throw papers away that I shouldn't throw away. I don't think he's right—but I can't find them anywhere. My organization has gone to hell and things are no longer in perfect order or anything like it and they don't get back into order till I start the next year. And then they don't stay in order. (But maybe it's just my fourth husband isn't very neat around the house.)

It was four years after my third husband died—and a year or so before all this happened with Andrew and the bongs—my present husband and I were married, and I suspect I am just as difficult as I ever was but he seems to be more tolerant (except when he loses his temper). But we still fight, and he hates it. You see, I'm writing—or rather dictating—this on an upswing—otherwise it wouldn't be written (or dictated) at all. But he keeps getting involved in writing projects of his own, entries for topical encyclopedias or in essay collections, for publishers like ABC-Clio and Sage. But while I'm able to work on this, I grudge him any writing time spent on anything else. (His author's copy of the ABC-Clio encyclopedia on *Drugs and Alcohol in North America* arrived while he still had work to do in the next three weeks on the Sage *Encyclopedia of Alcohol: Social, Cultural, Historical Perspectives*—which was completed and the three volumes of that encyclopedia arrived as we were getting back to this after a long hiatus when I was sick again and he took a full-time job in Harrisburg.)

One problem is—when I'm onto something I have to be onto it. If the house needs to be cleaned (only in this part of the country they say "needs cleaned"), I have to get it cleaned, and I work myself almost into collapse to get it cleaned. He says he needs multiple projects and switching from one to another makes it possible for him to go on working without collapsing. And the other problem is—when I become more manic he becomes more withdrawn. When the weather isn't bad, he sometimes used to go for walks down to the bridge over the creek at the end of the next street (where we used to walk with Jeffrey); he says he meditates there. Last night I was so furious over his taking on a commitment to write some encyclopedia entries I wouldn't let him say prayers with me: I didn't want him around me at all.

Sometimes I forget there's something or someone (or Something or Someone) behind every move I make. When I can keep that thought in the forefront of my thinking, I do much better with everyone in my life—family, co-workers, others in A. A. Keeping that thought where it belongs—always present in my mind—comes out of my taking inventory. But there's an extra problem for someone who's shifting cyclically from up to down to up to down, with in-between periods of varying lengths. That's probably why the Tenth Step has proved difficult for me over the years, The following Step, the Eleventh, the "prayer and meditation" step, is another key in staying sober—and therefore, for me, making it possible to deal with my manic depression. But meditation is much harder for me than the prayer, because it means keeping my mind still.

My mind races when I'm "up" and seems to function almost not at all (sometimes) when I'm "down." Trying to meditate (when my mind was functioning), I would sit down, put my feet on the floor, my hands on my lap, and try to close my mind to the outside world. It never worked, though for these several years (we're in the 1970s) I tried and tried. And then, when I had "Big Book Mary" as my sponsor, I finally told her I just couldn't meditate. She said, "I think you can," and set out to prove I could.

I went over to her house. We sat down and we read from the "Big Book," and then I could sense her mind becoming quiet, and after a minute or two, mine began to quiet down, more than it ever had before. I leaned that, for me, it's much easier to practice the art of meditation in the company of another person or even several other people, than it is to do it alone. And I had learned that it isn't by trying to close my mind off (that doesn't help it function, even if I could do it voluntarily) but by letting it be opened up, that I could begin meditation.

("Big Book Mary" also had a technique involving "mental time travel" where I (or we if there were more than just Mary and me) would concentrate on being somewhere else in time (I remember the Low Countries, apparently in the Seventeenth Century, with wooden shoes): this, too, functioned to expand our reach-of-mind, I guess you'd call it.)

Some of the best stories of my early sobriety come from my years before I really became aware of the interplay of bipolarity and the process of sobriety—they aren't really particularly relevant here, unfortunately. I think of the lady who walked the streets in Philadelphia: I told her she needed a job with regular hours so she could regularly attend meetings. She got a job providing phone sex from an adult book store—but it had regular hours. (She would up going back to school and college, and getting at least her Master's degree, and teaching in the Sociology Department at one of the

Philadelphia [Catholic] colleges.)

All these are in relatively bright colors in my memory—and then in 1988, we moved from my familiar Philadelphia area to Central Pennsylvania, and the colors aren't as bright. I went on sponsoring women in A. A. Some have been a pleasure to work with—though they didn't always all of them stay sober, and some have been a pleasure because they stayed sober, but being their sponsor was sort of like taking medicine—it was good for me, and it worked, but it didn't taste good. And with some it simply didn't work out. There's one I simply had to refuse a call from (she was in prison in a state a thousand miles away) because I was very ill, on my way to the hospital—I've not heard from her since and that was a dozen years ago, though the Corrections site in her state tells me she's eligible for release this year, so perhaps I will hear from her again. (She is bipolar.)

When I was in my twenties—and alas! also my thirties—I thought that having all the information I had at my fingertips (more or less) would impress everyone with who I was. People resent know-it-alls. Next to not picking up a drink—and not giving my phone number to someone in A. A.—that may have been the hardest thing I had to learn. I thought that being a perfectionist was the way to go and people would be glad to know someone who strove so obviously for perfection. I was wrong. I'm not so much a perfectionist any more (at least not to the degree I was), and much of the time I let other people take the reins, and I hold back. I have to do this everywhere—even in my job (when I was still working). Perfectionism and "knowing-it-all" were defense mechanisms I had for not taking a really serious look at myself, because once I did take a real serious look at myself, these attitudes were no more attractive to me than they were to my associates and my family, in the fellowship (of A. A.), and at home.

Another thing—when I moved to Central Pennsylvania, I had to get a new sponsor—I've mentioned that already. We'll call her Geraldine (which was her name but not how she was usually called). She and her husband lived in a house close to three hundred years old, equidistant between the church where we went to Monday night meetings and where I live in the next town. I used to stop in and see her sometimes on non-meeting nights and she and her husband and I (and later my present husband) would have ice cream at their dining-room table. And I would suddenly run out of energy and almost fall asleep into my ice-cream.

It was my (present) husband who suggested this might be the result of whatever it is in my internal make-up that provides me with no gradual acceleration or deceleration in my internal engine—it tends to be full speed or full stop. How exactly this is related to my cyclothymia, my racing mind or mind stopped, I do not know—nor does he. But he is convinced of the relationship. And the full-speed or full-stop comes into my practicing these principles in all my affairs (A. A.'s Step Twelve). My bipolar condition doesn't make Step Twelve easier.

I've been remembering and looking over my bipolar life in (alcoholic) recovery, especially in the last twenty-plus years, when I was moved from what seemed to be the relatively even keel of my life in the Philadelphia area, with a familiar kind of A. A. in familiar surroundings, to unfamiliar Lancaster County, in Central Pennsylvania. My (third) husband had found a new job there: it was a good job, but the *there* was a lot different, and we both made somewhat heavy weather of it. Then, after less than four years, my husband was very ill (cancer) and died. Within two or three months, I had a call from my brother in Minnesota; his marriage had broken down; he and his wife had broken up; and she wanted nothing to do with him. He wanted to come live with me. He arrived in September, after my husband had died around the end of June.

I had hoped my brother's coming would bring back something of the spirit of the days when he and I (and my mother and Uncle Mike) went to meetings together in and around Philadelphia. My brother and I did go to many of the same meetings here in Central Pennsylvania, but he had somehow been wounded by his marriage and his move to his wife's home state in the Midwest, and my mother and Uncle Mike were dead, and we weren't in and around Philadelphia.

My brother and I were even living in the same house, but at best we were on parallel tracks, and somehow we'd get switched away from each other. I think maybe I was "up" when he came, but then quickly I was on the way down, and the decline became greater when things didn't go quite as I had anticipated. And not long after he came, it began to be apparent he wasn't physically well—indeed, within a year he was showing major signs of the lung cancer that killed him just about a year after that. He came to meetings almost up to the very end. He was fifty-one.

Meanwhile, I became involved in the group affairs of the Thursday-Friday Group, became the General Service Representative (G.S.R.) for that group—which means I went to the monthly General Service District meeting over in Lititz. This may be too much A. A. detail, but the point is, I went with my good friend Grace, who was G.S.R. for our Tuesday Night Step Group—and what happened was that the sense of fellowship I really wanted was not with me and my brother but with me and Grace and her friend JoAnne and my sponsor Gerri (Geraldine), all of them, by the way, older than I, Grace and Gerri by a generation, and JoAnne by close to that.

It was about the time my term as G.S.R. was up that Teddy went into the hospital (again) to come out only to die two months later. He died April 1st and every year about that time—but certainly not only about that time—I think about him more, wondering what I could have done to make things work out better. The five or six months after his death were one of the worst periods in my life. I didn't seem to be able to do things right. Or sometimes simply to do things. Full-speed or full-stop, again.

Of course, that sounds like a manic-depressive episode, and it could have been—but I didn't think they were supposed to be "triggered" and this seemed to be. But perhaps the immediate connection with my brother's death was coincidental. In any case, my son was still going to N. A. meetings with his ride, and his driver and I went to A. A. meetings together—and when he had the required two years' sobriety, my sponsor had him voted in as G.S.R. at "her" meeting down the road in Mount Joy, that had been without a G.S.R. for a while. We went there on Monday nights, to our Elizabethtown Step Meeting on Tuesday nights, Hershey on Wednesdays, Elizabethtown on Thursdays and Fridays, and Hershey most Saturdays. Sundays we mostly went to church. And then in September [September 21, 1996] we were married at the little church we had been attending in Mount Joy.

But before that happened, I had my first attack of Giant-Cell Arteritis, and temporarily lost the sight in my left eye. I was ordered by my optometrist to an ophthalmologist and by him to a neuro-ophthalmologist at Hershey Medical Center who had written a medical-journal study on Neuro-ophthalmalogical effects of Giant-Cell Arteritis. After emergency treatment with cortico-steroids my left-eye vision was largely restored, at least temporarily. This was in August; my (fourth) marriage was in September. Almost everyone at the wedding (except a few extended family members) was A. A., except my husband's best man (an old college friend) and two groomsmen (his nephew Chris and an old graduate-school friend). My son gave me away.

It wasn't long thereafter my husband was asked to be his District's Committeeman on A. A.'s Area [Eastern Pennsylvania] Committee. I had become our Hershey Group's G.S.R., and then became their District's Alternate Area Committeewoman (though they say "Committee Member" to avoid identifying gender). I know this sounds (1) confusing and (2) boring—even to people in A. A. service, but these committees are the way people in A. A. get together and work with other people in A. A. to set up the structure that enables A. A. groups to relate to—and work with—each other. (It may be based on 1930s political party structure.)

In 1999, while serving as District Committeewoman I was nominated for a position as Appointed Committee Member on the [New York] Trustees' Committee on Correctional Facilities, because of long sobriety, longtime service including taking meetings into correctional facilities, and my current position with the Pennsylvania Department of Corrections.. I think I was in an "up" phase—my son seemed to have come through his troubles—and when my husband drove me up to New York, I was interviewed and appointed to the Committee beginning in May 2000, and tapped to speak at a Workshop on A. A. and the Criminal Justice System at the International Convention in Minneapolis (a city I have loved from the time I was an airline stewardess).

Working at the training academy was interesting (if not generally as interesting as SCI-Camp Hill); I set up courses for new hires and people who were promoted and I had some inmate contact—principally with good-behavior inmates serving in the dining room and kitchen at the Training Academy. My big surprise was being able to take a firearms course. I didn't do well with the long guns because they were too heavy and too long for me, but I passed the small arms course. Remember, by this time I was fifty-three. I couldn't get to the long-arms target and I couldn't get the gun up—it was too heavy. But with the handguns I did very well, got to the target directly as advertised.

I remember working there at the Academy the day of 9/11. When we came in, we were all given red-white-and-blue ribbons and went to the auditorium where we sang songs like "God Bless America," and "America the Beautiful," and "Amazing Grace." One thing about my time at the Training Academy, I recall it as a good pleasant day-to-day job—except that I would sometimes rush around, trying to get done in a single day what would and should have taken two days (or been done in one day by two people). I think that's important. My husband thinks that's very important—and he thinks that it's connected to my vasculitis. I suppose it might be. I've almost always had a kind of manic haste and impatience in my life, sometimes weaker, sometimes stronger.

All the sudden new dimension to my service in A. A. made me wonder a little, but I kept up my work at the Department of Corrections Training Academy, and my A. A. New York work, and going to my regular meetings, and serving as District Committee-woman on the [Eastern Pennsylvania] Area Committee, and having my grandson several days and nights a week to take him to his pre-school and then kindergarten and the Susquehanna Waldorf School.

My husband and I shared getting Jeffrey to and from school and my husband drove me to my District meetings and my quarterly Area Committee meetings at the four corners of Eastern Pennsylvania and to New York for my quarterly meetings there. And when I was up in New York at the Quarterly Trustees' Committee meeting in April 2002, I came down with a flu-type sickness, and pretty much collapsed. I made it through most of the physical sickness in a couple of weeks (but I remember having to make extra stops on the way back to Pennsylvania). Even with the physical sickness pretty much over, I felt depressed and tired—in fact the depression may have been there before we went up to New York. That month had begun with the seventh anniversary of my brother's death.

I wouldn't give in to the "tired." And I worked harder and harder at the Training Academy. I kept up with the District Committee-woman position. Except my husband had to fill in for me at two of the 2002 Quarterly Area meetings. Then my Giant-Cell Arteritis (CNS Vasculitis) kicked in again, the sight in my left eye went away again, and my health broke down pretty completely. I managed to get up to New York to the October 2002 Trustees' meeting, but by December I was on temporary medical leave from work (they had to get two people in to cover for me), and my husband had to fill in for me at District meetings (he was a G.S.R. in my district) and then was elected to succeed me in December 2002. I know now that my activities with all I had to do had passed into the manic, but it had been disguised from me by the hovering presence of depression— and when my husband suggested I might be trying to do too much, I couldn't listen—couldn't hear him.

You see, one of my problems in being severely bipolar is that when I'm down, or going down, I know it and want to increase my medication (in my case back to the original 900 mg of lithium per day)> But when I'm up, even if I'm irritable, I don't recognize the "up" and will insist I'm fine. Fortunately, my sobriety was good enough that I didn't drink during all this time—as far as I know didn't even come close—but somehow I didn't always seem to be practicing all A. A.'s principles in all my affairs.

We have slogans to help keep us on the beam—"Easy Does it"— "One Day at a Time"—I wasn't listening well. I wasn't listening well to that part of our Serenity Prayer where it says. "Grant me the serenity to accept those things I cannot change"—serenity wasn't in me (and I think I thought I could change everything). The people at my work were saying they didn't know how I could do all the things I was doing—and even our high-school intern thought I was going too fast too much. And then the collapse came.

I made to some of my regular meetings. I was out of my responsibilities as a District Committeewoman. I made it to the end-of-January/beginning-of-February Trustees' Committee meeting in New York, and I seemed to be recovered sufficiently (although now legally blind) to go back to work in March. My husband drove me to work and picked me up. But the medicines I was taking, and my fatigue, combined to make me so sleepy I couldn't guarantee to stay awake at my desk even for a morning. And in May 2003 came the decision I had dreaded: I had to retire on complete disability. And it wasn't safe for me to drive any longer. The last time I drove a car was six blocks to my dentist and six back one June afternoon in 2003.

I went to my last few New York Trustees' meetings through April 2004, though I don't think I was very far along on my long climb back to (relative) physical health. I could still speak at meetings when I was in relatively good shape, but it was dicey. This Central Nervous System Vasculitis (Giant-Cell Arteritis) works like this: the system generates too many Giant Cells the kind that combat invading illnesses—and the extra cells start hardening against an artery well and blocking the blood flow—say, to the optic nerve. The left optic nerve is starved for blood, stops operating—and there I am, blind in my left eye. That happened to me in 1996 but it could be reversed. It happened in 2002 and couldn't be. But the symptoms of Giant-Cell Arteritis mimic the symptoms of Parkinson's and lithium toxicity, and sometimes just plain fatigue—and, more dangerously for the manic depressive mimic or exacerbate the symptoms of bipolar disorder activity.

It was after I'd been retired for disability about a year that I began dictating my first book to my husband. That was relatively easy: it was a Q & A book on alcoholism and sobriety, and I'd been praying and thinking and working hard in A. A. for going on forty years for over thirty years, including making use of at least one previous Q & A book on the subject. And I wasn't doing much A. A. service work. But then I was asked to help restore a "dark" District in A. A. and wound up volunteering to serve as their Committeewoman for a year. But then the colleague who was supposed to replace me couldn't do it, and I was asked to serve another two years, and the fatigue closed in. And the "down." Finally a former committeeman from an adjacent district volunteered, and I was out from under, and I could get started on this book.

One of the things that slowed us down on this book was that my bipolar life has been the bipolar life of an alcoholic centering on recovery from alcoholism. It's not meant to be exclusive—I believe any manic depressive or friend or loved one of a manic depressive can benefit, but it is written by an alcoholic manic-depressive whose goal in the forty-five years since she received her diagnosis as bipolar (manic depressive) has been sobriety. And that's bound to color things.

So we've spent a lot of time trying to balance value to all manic depressives with (or against) value especially to manic depressive alcoholics (or alcoholic manic depressives). And then for a couple of years my husband had a job where he was away from the house twelve hours a day as against the six-to-eight for teaching, But finally we're here (just now on the last re-ordering and run-through). Let me step back briefly to a day four years ago.

Suddenly it was October (2013), and I was coming up on my forty-third Anniversary in A. A. I was asked to speak at the Hershey Group First Saturday Speakers' Meeting on my exact Anniversary, and once again I was "up" for a commitment. My husband was chairing—he gave me my Forty-three year "chip" (medal), then said "You're on!" and I gave the best talk I'd given in years (and I haven't done as well since), ending with a standing ovation from a full crowd. Somehow, with that brief introduction after getting my "chip"—and no time for doubt to build up—the memories of successful talks of long ago, and my happiness at being out from under in the service job, and my just feeling good again, all brought phrases to my mind that I hadn't used in telling my story for years. It all fit together in my mind—and though one of the effects of CNS Vasculities is aphasia where you forget the word you were aiming for and go on helplessly repeating the words leading up to it, that didn't happen to me that night. I found a substitute for the one word I couldn't reach, and I did it without repeating the run-up.

Now that was almost four years ago, and I haven't spoken as well since. I'm mostly down to three or four meetings a week. I'm getting along on the reduced lithium intake and am hoping that maybe my system is adjusting—maybe at age 76 I'm just slowing down. (I am, however, having more and more trouble drinking enough fluid to keep my lithium retention levels down—at least sixty-four ounces a day, which is actually a "normal" level for anyone.) It still bothers me I can't drive. The last twenty years have been very different in many ways from my life before—and the one before that. And how my alcoholic condition interacts with my whole bipolar life. is particularly important for this book—and I have come to see how my manic depression (bipolarity) shows in my whole life course, and how it interacts with my alcoholism and recovery from alcoholism.

For most of my sober life I treated my "manic depression" as an outside issue, separate from my alcoholism and recovery from alcoholism—but as more and more women I sponsored said (and convinced me) they were bipolar, or even hearing those I didn't sponsor share at meetings, I began to see that I couldn't fully keep them apart. I couldn't share much of this at meetings, because for non-bipolar alcoholics it really is an outside issue, apart from the business of A. A. meetings, which is sobriety for alcoholics, not any specific and separated variety of alcoholics.

It may be simply that I'm more attuned to "bipolarity" in alcoholics than I used to be, but I see it more and more. I'm only actively sponsoring one woman in A. A.—I think new members may be turned off by my age and long sobriety—but she is a "manic depressive" under doctor's treatment, though not with Lithium Carbonate (but that is very much an outside issue for A. A.). Right now my Twelfth-Step work is at a lower level than I would like—only this one active "pigeon" and no service positions, and I haven't spoken (like at my Forty-Third) for over a year, though I do try to share at most meetings I go to (every once in a while I lose my confidence to the prospect of aphasia).

Right now, if all goes well, I'm looking forward to telling my story at Hershey on Saturday, October 7, 2017, when I will get my forty-seven year medal ("chip") from my husband, who will be chairing the meeting. If nothing goes wrong in the next month. We're praying all will be well. In the words of the old prayer, "All will be well, and all will be well, and all manner of thing shall be well."

And yes, I pray in connection with my bipolar condition as well as my alcoholism. I wonder if it couldn't be cured by prayer, but I'm not sure I could even pray unaided by the Lithium. I'm not sure there's a praying right as against a praying wrong, but if there is—and I think there probably is—then in my experience depression can prevent it, and so can mania, even if it doesn't completely prevent prayer at all, of any kind.

If you had asked me a few years ago whether I really paid attention to how my bipolar condition affected my day-to-day life, I would have said, "Yes—of course." But my day-to-day life was concerned with my continuing recovery from alcoholism, and, as you see, I've only recently begun to consider the full extent of the intersection of my two (major) diseases, even though Dr. Zarate gave me the clue forty-five years ago. I don't know whether manic depressives who are not alcoholics don't fully analyze the way their bipolarity affects their life, and maybe analysis isn't necessary—but I think it is, and I suspect this is an area where all manic-depressives would benefit from more thought and less merely instinctive reaction. After all, men—or women—who object to reduced sexual drive might want to consider whether sexual drive is all that makes life worth living, and take lithium rather than winding up committing suicide.

Possibly a new drug will come along, out of anti-craving experiments (like those producing Naltrexone) or anti-opioid experiments (Narcan)—but then it may be highly addictive (or at least habituating)—more and more needed for less and less in result. Maybe virtual reality experiments will produce some kind of treatment related to ECT and/or the "white light" experience—only it will make you sick to your stomach, and you may wind up like the teenager who couldn't distinguish between himself and his character in Dungeons & Dragons—and finally chose to live in D&D (in an institution for a while until he was able to change his choice). I'm not basing my life course on what might possibly happen.

Before going on to talk about the bipolar condition and what I believe I understand about it. I want to mention an "up" and a "down" from my early experience with the Pennsylvania DOC, and then a couple of characteristic experiences in the far reaches of my manic (bipolar) condition—that stick by me and with me though I'm not sure why, nor what they mean. First, for my DOC experience. After HACC, I worked at a temporary agency—I was only there in a job a few days when someone asked me if I wanted to apply for a job at Camp Hill Prison. Of course I was thrilled. I applied there and just about the next day was working in the office of the inmate program manager. I was a temporary worker for a while and then I became a permanent employee at the Pennsylvania Department of Corrections. The person I worked for was highly respected throughout the prison and I was extremely grateful to be working for him.

But—I started my first day, and where was my boss? Then they got the phone call and they told me where he was. You see, my boss was never late—that's what his secretary said (and I found out later she was right)—but today he was late. The night before, his six-year-old son, who had a baby kitten, wanted to sleep out in a tent in the backyard with the kitten, and the kitten kept getting out of the tent, and the little boy kept coming in to his father for help, so finally he went out and retrieved the kitten from wherever he had gone, and the three of them, my boss and his little boy and his little boy's kitten, all slept out in the tent in the back yard.

I was convinced then and there—and I have remained convinced the twenty years since —that I had the best of all possible bosses. That first day was a high point in my time at SCI-Camp Hill—and I'll tell you about the low point.

One day I was looking out the window and I saw a man coming through the gate in shackles; I had never seen shackles before and I remember thinking this must be what they call man's inhumanity to man. I knew the man had committed crimes and he needed to be in prison—I understood that but I didn't understand the shackles around ankles, legs, feet, and chest—of course I couldn't tell anyone how I felt because they wouldn't understand how I didn't understand. That night I prayed for that man and I prayed for many like him, for many nights.

I can still see him—not the face but coming through the sally-gate shackled. At first I didn't know what they were and then I knew. Some of the work at SCI-Camp Hill was preparing pre-parole documentation. It was very detailed work; it was extremely interesting. I did not have any inmate contact there, even though I was technically "behind the walls"—I had a private office upstairs over Control with a big office window. I worked at Camp Hill for a while, but we had only one car then, and it was a long drive, twenty-nine miles in thirty-four minutes, and then my husband had to drive to his job back in Harrisburg, back across the Susquehanna, again. There was an opening at the DOC Training Academy in Elizabethtown, a few minutes from my house.

The other important thing—when I switched from Camp Hill to the Training Academy, it made me more available for my newly-discovered grandson. And I'm someone who would rather spend my time with a child, almost any child, rather than with anyone else. This is a key to my remembering this second set of memories—even though they do not all involve Andrew or Jeffrey. But I think they're related.

When Andrew was growing up I read to him constantly. We played games, went for walks, took trips to the Jersey Shore and New England, and the Philadelphia Zoo and museums including the Philadelphia Art Museum, you know, the "Rocky" one. We took trips to Vermont and to the Maryland and Delaware shore and to the Jersey shore—Avalon, where I grew up in the summers. I had no trouble driving to and from Avalon, but when I took Andrew up to a spiritual retreat in Vermont—when he was less than a year old—this was what happened.

It turned out that we all—adults, children, babies—slept in a single big room, on cots, only Andrew didn't sleep—he cried and cried and cried all night. I couldn't get him to stop crying, so I went to the retreat person and said, "I can't have Andrew upset like this and I have to get him home to his own room."

Next morning I picked up my car and my baby and all our equipment, and I was driving back to Pennsylvania, and all of a sudden I was lost. Somehow I found out where I was—what town (I knew I was still in Vermont, I think, but by that time it might have been Massachusetts: wherever it was, it wasn't where I wanted to be)—and I was crying and my baby was crying.

I called my second husband, actually then my second ex-husband, and he told me to find the bus station in the town and wait for him there: he couldn't fly up or take a train, and he couldn't drive, because then there would be two cars and one driver, so he took the bus up to rescue me. By the time I got through to him I had started to calm down. I rested and my baby rested, and we calmed down some more, and I found the bus station, and I pulled up, and after a while, there he was, and we came home. This was several years after our divorce, and I've thought how extraordinarily lucky I was that his concern for me or my baby or both brought him to my aid from five states away. (No, he did not want to remarry me.)

The second time I had trouble on a longer-distance drive was about ten years later, when Andrew and I went down to the shore— but not the Jersey shore. I was in Delaware, on I-95, and somehow I was convinced I was going the wrong way. Actually, now, many years after, I'm not sure, but I know that I pulled over and used one of those emergency phones they had to have at the roadside: Andrew was mortified—he tried to talk me out of it. We had the dog in the car (it was the blue Oldsmobile we had until early 1995)—the dog was Bandit, our Sheltie, a really neat dog—and Bandit was barking. So the State Trooper came, and I said, "I know you have better things to do than take care of someone who's all confused about where she is and which way she's going."

And he said, "Ma'am, my job right now is to get you and your boy and your dog on your way back to Pennsylvania," and he did just that, staying behind us till he knew we couldn't make a mistake and were unalterably headed back to Pennsylvania. That would have been about 1991 or maybe 1992. But I've continued from time to time to have this kind of trouble. When my grandson came along it was the same thing all over again about taking him places—the same thing as with my son. I spent as much time with him as I could. We used to take walks down to the bridge at the end of the next street—there were horses in a pasture further over and we used to go "see the horsies." (I used to be able to walk more than a few steps then.)

He doesn't remember it—he's twenty-two and it was eighteen or nineteen years ago—but I do. We had him in a Waldorf school [or pre-school] in Marietta and my husband would drive him in the morning and I would take my lunch hour to pick him up (I was now at the Academy), or if I couldn't, my husband would—but it was thirty miles longer roundtrip for him from Harrisburg.

We remember Jeffrey's looking in a barn door we went by on the way to the Waldorf School to see if the red tractor was in there—but he doesn't remember it. If we had driven that road with him in the years between, and mentioned it to him, he would probably remember remembering it—but we didn't, and his whole memory of it seems to be lost. Do we remember things as they were?

Sometimes a memory can be reinforced—or at least brought out of retirement—by something that happens later. It was about ten years after that time on the Delaware Turnpike, when I was married to my fourth and present husband that I took an A. A. meeting into the Cumberland County Jail in Carlisle, on the west shore of the Susquehanna: my husband wasn't with me.

He had given me careful directions about getting on the Pennsylvania Turnpike coming back from Carlisle to the east shore where we live, and I had done it several times before, recently. But this time my arteritis attacks had started and my sight was getting worse) I wound up going west, next exit Blue Mountain. I pulled over to the side of the road—the turnpike there has wide shoulders—and started to cry. A State trooper came up.

He listened to me and then he told me, "Ma'am, don't ever let anyone know I'm doing this," and he guided me onto the restricted access road to the State Police Office there, and I called my husband and he and my son came down and got me, and my son drove my car back. I don't suppose it was significant that these happened at ten-year intervals, and when ten years from the last one had passed I was no longer driving, so it couldn't happen again.

But I do know that recently—about ten years from the last episode—I have looked up on familiar streets around home, with my husband driving, and not known where I was. So this recent memory reinforces others longer ago, and I see a continuing pattern. One thing puzzles me. I read about the experiences of other manic depressives, and they seem more vivid than mine. I wonder if it has to do with my being one of those manic depressives who took to alcohol as self-medication.

Now for some questions. We had four major questions on the cover: Let's take a look at them now.

The original first question was, what is it like to live a bipolar life? I hope what you have read thus far helps illuminate the answer to that question, at least so far as my own bipolar life is concerned. We have three major questions left, with a sub-question under Treatment:

1) What is Manic Depression (Bipolar condition)?
2) How can it be treated? How can we live with it?
3) How it is related to alcoholism?

Q&A:
MANIC DEPRESSION /BIPOLAR CONDITION

Here are four questions--as amended, one might say–though one of them doesn't sound exactly like a *question*.

QUESTION 1: WHAT IS MANIC DEPRESSION?
QUESTION 2: HOW CAN IT BE TREATED?
QUESTION 3: VISION/DREAM? VR? CURE W/IN?
QUESTION 4: BIPOLAR/ALCOHOLIC LINKS?

QUESTION 1: WHAT IS MANIC DEPRESSION?

I thought back in 1970-71 that I was simply a recovering alcoholic who would become a recovered alcoholic and have a life of meetings and service and doing the Twelve. It wasn't to be that simple—no, I didn't say *easy*, I said *simple*.

All these ups and downs in my life are still under the care of a doctor and medication—what would it be like if they weren't? But right now we need to talk about just what this manic depression—bipolar-I—bipolar-II—cyclothymia—is. Let me begin by drawing four boxes, one for each classification from more serious to less serious, moving left to right. Then, on the following pages we will look within the boxes, at defining characteristics, moving left to right.

MANIC DEPRESSION	BIPOLAR-I	BIPOLAR-II	CYCLO-THYMIA

And here are the details:

FIRST BOX: MANIC DEPRESSION

Symptoms of Mania

Much less need for sleep
Exaggerated inappropriate happiness
Inappropriate grandiosity
Exaggerated self-esteem
Unrealistic beliefs about one's own powers
More energy than normal
Exaggerated talkativeness/Racing thoughts
Hypersexuality

Symptoms of Depression
Exaggerated sadness/fearfulness
No ability to enjoy things
No desire to be with family or friends
Withdrawal/isolation
No motivation to do things one used to enjoy
Tiredness/low energy
Poor performance at school or work
Wishing one were dead
Thoughts of suicide/even attempts at suicide

Distinguishing Qualitative Characteristics

"Mixed-Manic" States (Manic and Depressive Conditions)

Note that these terms and conditions are more conversational and less quantitative than those for the succeeding degrees of illness defined as Bipolar-I, Bipolar-II, and Cyclothymia, and also that the definition of the condition overlaps that of Bipolar-I.

It will be remarked, I think—certainly I have remarked it—that some of the words defining these conditions are frequently used to describe characteristics of alcoholics—for example, grandiosity, exaggerated self-esteem, isolation/withdrawal, alienation from family. This first list of (overlapping) characteristics is pretty rudimentary and represents mostly what I learned when I was first diagnosed as manic-depressive.

I'm not posing here as an expert on bipolar disorder, but I have many decades of experience living my bipolar life (if that's what I should call it), and when I was first diagnosed—and since then—I read everything I could find on this disease I had—and have.

For those who aren't bi-polar (in my case also and originally called manic depressive), or those who may be but haven't studied it, I can tell you there's some agreement on what the disorder—or psychosis—is, not so much on how it's best treated. And my experience pretty much bears out what I read back then, and since.

This is a kind of layman's account, emphasizing symptoms, before going on to the distinctions between and among manic depression (a term still used, though not so widely as it once was), bipolar disorder I (bipolar-I), bi-polar disorder II (bipolar-II), and cyclothymia (which is a term, more or less, for the weak form of the disease – but I should still emphasize that the various degrees of the disease do not differ only in strength: there are qualitative differences, from all I know from experience and have been told).

I wondered at first why it was called manic depression (and I sometimes wonder why it isn't—mostly—called manic depression any more. To me, "bipolar-I" is just weak, or sounds weak.) As I have just now been saying, manic depression is not really neatly divided into manic and depressive states, nor is the manic state particularly different from other manic states, nor is the depressive state neatly separated from other depressive states.

In fact, so far as I know, the manic state is not neatly divided from depression generally. The combined term "manic depressive psychosis" covers the bubbling shifting nature of the disease, the possibility that mania develops so naturally out of depression that it might almost be considered an advanced form of depression (a point made by Kay Redfield Jamison in her book, *An Unquiet Mind*)—and she is herself a manic depressive.

The combined term covers the frequent occurrence of mixed manic or angry manic states (seeming to combine both mania and depression), and fact that what seem to be normal states are in fact unstable points on the passages between mania and depression. In other words, the "normal" is that there really is no normal. And all appearances of "normal" phases should be handled very carefully, with a sense that "things are not what they seem."

Not only is it not true that all passages from mania to depression or depression to mania are through a more "normal" period. What has been particularly true for me has been that periods of passage from depression to mania have had no "normalcy" about them. For me, all passages from one state to the other, but particularly these, seem to combine both states.

This is one of the reasons that it seems to me from my experience, as to Dr. Jamison from hers, that the word "bi-polar" much too neatly ties off one state from the other. This book is written to share with manic depressives puzzling about their lives (or others puzzling about them) to let them—and you—know about my life.

Because I am that common kind of manic depressive who is also an alcoholic, the book has something on the inter-relationship of the two. Because Dr. Jamison reports that sixty percent of alcoholics are bipolar, and the other way 'round, it seems to me reasonable to look at the overlapping condition and would be even if it didn't apply to me. (But it does, which makes it easier for me to talk about.)

I have read about the manic states other manic depressives have had—great fun, high enthusiasms, and long runs of very hard but enjoyable work. I have read about starting out to buy one book and buying twenty that all seemed magically related.

Then the manic phase would end and the manic depressive could only stare at and dread the day and occasionally pointlessly rearrange the books, but never accomplish anything of value, refuse to answer door or phone, living in what Jude, in the New Testament, calls "the blackness of darkness forever." (Maybe he was manic-depressive.)

SECOND BOX: BIPOLAR I

- A distinct period of abnormally and persistently elevated, expansive or irritable mood lasting at least seven days [hypomanic four days]

- During the period of mood disturbance at least three of the following symptoms persistently present to a significant degree [four if mood is only irritable]: [a] inflated self-esteem [grandiosity]; [b] decreased need for sleep; [c] more talkative than usual or pressure to keep talking; [d] insomnia or hypersomnia nearly every day; [e] psychomotor agitation or retardation nearly every day [observable by others]; [f] flight of ideas or subjective feelings, are racing, distractibility; [g] increased goal-directed activity [social/sexual/school/work] or psychomotor agitation]; heavy involvement in pleasure activities with high potential for painful consequences.

- The symptoms do not meet criteria for a Mixed Episode.

- The mood disturbance is sufficiently severe to cause marked impairment in occupational functioning or social activities/relationships or to necessitate hospitalization to prevent harm to self or others.

- The symptoms are not due to the direct physiological effects of a substance (e.g., a medication) or a general medical condition (e.g., hyperthyroidism).

- That for the hypomanic episode there must be a mood disturbance and change in functioning, observable by others, but Criterion 4 does not apply.

Psychoses and disorders are defined by the *DSM* (*Diagnostic and Statistical Manual*, details given for manic and hypomanic episodes in what *DSM-IV* calls bipolar disorder (manic depression). Here are the qualifications for Bipolar-I from the *Manual*—the fourth edition—*DSM-IV*—being the best known, though we now have a fifth). We should probably write that definition down here, in our box, though it's scarcely easy going.

The thing that strikes me, when I read this out of the *DSM-IV*, is that they spend a lot of time on the manic and even hypomanic [=less manic] episodes, and not much on the depressive. Maybe everyone knows what depression is, and it *is* defined in the *DSM-IV*. Apparently the pole that is particularly important in my bipolar world (or at least to observers of my bipolar world) is the manic.

What creates this manic depressive psychosis? There seems to be a genetic predisposition (I learned about those with alcohol and alcoholism), suggesting there is an inheritable chemical imbalance—almost certainly in one or more of the neurotransmitters in the brain, most likely (it was first thought) norepinephrine, though I haven't heard that very much lately. The four major neurotransmitters, I learned, are norepinephrine, dopamine, acetylcholine, and serotonin. All four are implicated in manic depression, though in different ways. (By the way, recent research on the feminine libido suggests that serotonin is, for women's sexuality, something of a "downer.")

A shortage of norepinephrine in the system is linked to depressive states. In my study of alcoholism I learned that alcohol, which is generally thought of as a depressant, in fact aids in boosting norepinephrine into the system, at least up to a point. (We apparently don't really know what that point is.) A substantial reduction in dopamine transmission has been likewise thought to characterize the depressive phase, though it may not be the quantity so much as the ease of transmission that is of interest for the manic depressive. I learned in my study of alcoholism that alcohol intake reduces acetylcholine levels. Finally, it seems that (along with the matter of the feminine libido) the more serotonin in the manic depressive's system, the more rapid the shifts up to down to up.

The other kind of cause is the cause of the *onset* of the bipolar (or manic-depressive) condition. Onset, once the condition is established, could be "triggered" by some outside force or circumstance. (The shifts from high to low to high are generally not "triggered" but periodic. But the periods may be speeded up or slowed down through serotonin levels and blockers, or perhaps in other ways.) Among those triggers most often suggested were various kinds of abuse (physical, sexual, emotional) and loss of a loved one (particularly early loss of a parent). Other suggested triggers include childbirth, steroids, other drugs—but these do not cause condition or precondition, only trigger it into action.

Of course, if the condition (or precondition) is a chemical imbalance, then any substance that would increase the imbalance could trigger the active response. It seems that, in effect, my bipolar isn't exactly your bipolar, even if we are both bipolar-I, and even if we have the same family heritage. (This always holds, unless of course we are identical twins, and even then, one of us must be older and one younger, so not precisely identical in our life-events.) What chemicals adversely alter our chemical balance is unsure.

In any case, this triggering of the condition or precondition into activity is not the same thing as triggering a particular manic or depressive or mixed-manic episode. The more I read, and the more I looked at my own life, the more I realized that, once the pattern itself was started (and that was triggered), these episodes weren't triggered—they just were.

But what separates manic depression (or the overlapping bipolar-I disorder) from bipolar-II disorder from "simple" cyclothymia (if there is such a thing)? Let's set out the characteristics of Bipolar-II. Once again, this is not simply a weaker version of Bipolar-I, although it is partly that—just as Bipolar-I is not simply a weaker version of the old Manic Depression, though it seems partly that. But the actual sets of conditions, are not the same. Manic Depression has more mixed-manic states than Bipolar-I. Bipolar-I has more downs vs. ups than Bipolar-II.

THIRD BOX: BIPOLAR II

- The patient has had at least one major depressive episode lasting at least two weeks and at least one hypomanic episode lasting at least four days, but never had a manic episode. Major depressive episodes or unpredictable changes in mood and behavior cause distress or difficulty in areas of the subject's life.

- Having anxiety, feeling keyed up, tense or restless, trouble concentrating because fearing something awful may happen, or inability to control oneself

- Loss of pleasure in all or most activities and not feeling significantly better, even when something good happens—but atypically experiencing symptoms that are not typical of a major depressive episode, such as *having* a significantly improved mood when something good happens

- Catatonia—not reacting to environment, holding body in an unusual position, not speaking, or mimicking another person's speech or movement

- Triggered responses, such as postpartum depression or seasonal depressive patterns like those of "seasonal affective disorder"

Some of this is characteristic of Bipolar-I, but some of it (including absence of strong manic episodes) is definitely not. A slightly wider definition of Bipolar-II includes some mania (this may be a symptom of a desire to simplify—and unify—definitions, regardless of whether the distinctions are justified. Even so, this simplified definition says that the answer (as to how I and II diverge) is in the frequency and severity of the episodes and the rapidity of the shift. One characteristic separating bipolar-I from bipolar-II is the greater frequency (in that area of bipolar-I we call manic depression) of mixed manic or angry [irritable] manic episodes. But this refers only to a part of bipolar-I when the term itself is (confusingly?) extended to cover manic depression. Let's take a look at the distinctions between bipolar I and bipolar II, and what separates them both from simple cyclothymia.

In Bipolar-I the patient has had at least one manic episode. The manic episode may be preceded by or followed by hypomanic or major depressive episodes. Mania symptoms cause significant impairment in life processes and may require hospitalization or trigger a break from reality (psychosis). In Bipolar-II the patient has had at least one major depressive episode lasting at least two weeks and at least one hypomanic episode lasting at least four days, but never had a manic episode. Major depressive episodes or the unpredictable changes in mood and behavior can cause distress or difficulty in areas of the subject's life. So far—not bad. But one of the things we need to know is whether the conditions, manic depression, bipolar-I, bipolar-II, and cyclothymia (which we haven't come to yet), are similar in their origins and chemical characteristics—both psychologically and physiologically similar.

The biggest question, to my mind, is whether the lesser strength (as I think of it) of cyclothymia or cyclothymic disorder [1] provides a condition for different treatment and [2] whether in any other way there is a difference not simply quantitative (less strength) but qualitative (different in kind). Let's look at the Mayo Clinic characteristics of cyclothymia (or cyclothymic disorder), with some addition of characteristics given us in *DSM-IV*. In general, there does not seem to be any qualitative difference in Cyclothymia from Bipolar-I or II.

Just to summarize briefly, Cyclothymia may be of briefer duration than Bipolar-I or Bipolar-II—which of course means that it may be more often diagnosed in children and teenagers, who have had less time for anything to last. On the other hand because the symptoms are likely to less evident and children and teens are harder to diagnose than adults, it may often be suspectable but not capable of being fully diagnosed.

FOURTH BOX: CYCLOTHYMIA

At least two years—one for children/teenagers—of hypomania and depression

Symptoms less severe than full hypomanic or depressive episode

Symptoms occurring at least half the time and never long absent

Ups and Downs not as severe as Bipolar-I or -II

Feeling of stability between periods of up and down shifts of mood

High and Low symptoms can still interfere with patient's ability to function

High and Low symptoms and states seem to increase risk of Bipolar-I or -II

Cyclothymia less resistant to talk therapy (psychotherapy)

Continued contact with doctor for medication may provide form of talk therapy

---

The highs of cyclothymia produce symptoms of an elevated mood similar to bipolar symptoms (hypomanic symptoms). The lows consist of mild or moderate depressive symptoms. These symptoms are less severe than those of bipolar I or II disorder. A cyclothymic can typically function in daily life, though not always well.

The unpredictable nature of the mood shifts may greatly disrupt daily life since cyclothymics never know how they will feel.

It's important to remember that, even though cyclothymia may be "mild," the difficulty and even heartbreak brought about this unpredictability is scarcely unimportant–and may be disastrous–to the cyclothymic.

QUESTION 2: HOW CAN IT BE TREATED?

This "Treatment" section gets into some areas beyond the normal bounds of medicine—though perhaps less so as time goes on. It gets into matters like white-light dreams, a kind of "big dreams" (Carl Jung's term), *The Varieties of Religious Experience* (William James), and even Virtual Reality—besides, of course, going into other medications besides lithium.

BRIEF NOTE ON PROBLEMS WITH LITHIUM—AND TIPS

My own treatment for Bipolar Disorder, since 1972, has been Lithium therapy—the administration of Lithium Carbonate: discussion of this takes up most of the chapter. But there are other treatments, with other drugs, and these are becoming more popular—and other drugs are sometimes used to supplement lithium. We look at difficulties in finding other drugs or treatments for manic depression, a subject that could easily be taken as the occasion for very black humor. My condition as a manic depressive who is also alcoholic means these drugs are, as the doctors say, "contraindicated" in my case. But there are problems with Lithium, particularly as it affects sexual drive. Also, much easier to deal with, anyone using lithium is told to drink plenty of water every day—I was told that forty-five years ago, and it's still true today. Doctors often recommend a little extra salt with meals.

LITHIUM ALTERNATIVES

The older lithium alternatives are mostly either Thorazine (with its infamous "Thorazine shuffle") or very close to it. No, thank you. There is also—for both Manic Depression and Clinical (Major) Depression—what used to be called Shock Treatments, now going under the innocuous initials ECT (which, however, stands for electro-*convulsive* therapy —and that I also received). Some of the medicines used against bipolar I are anticonvulsants—but ECT produces convulsive shocks. Is there confusion here? Are there good convulsions and bad convulsions? Do we really know what we're doing? (I have to believe we do, but it's my mind and brain, and it's a little hard sometimes.) In any case, I cannot speak from my own experience of good results for Electro-Convulsive Therapy.

TWO KINDS OF DEPRESSIONS AND OTHER "BI-POLARITY"

I have noticed that I have had two kinds of depressions, what appear to be what I could call regular or gentle, and what seem to be extremely violent depressions. These tend to be depressions generally from three to six months apart. When I started the final work-through on this book, my last depression had been about eight months before, so I was feeling that these were becoming less difficult, less violent and I didn't know how long this eight months gap would last. (I sometimes believe I can feel the depressive shift coming on—but then I have to be careful I don't make that into a kind of self-fulfilling prophecy.)

If you, the reader, keep track of your depressions and mood swings (or those of your loved one), I should tell you there will be value in it for you (or him or her). The first doctor who put me on lithium told me to keep record whether my day was an eight or whatever (on a scale of one-to-ten) on the calendar. I did it for twenty years, then I stopped. Now (after another twenty) I've started again. I wish I'd kept it up, though I can at least remember something of the record I kept long ago.

I have thought of "bipolar" from various angles—that one of the things about bi-polar is I never know what I'm going to get. Over forty-plus years there's nothing that's been exactly the same every time around. I could say truthfully now—it seems to me—that most of my life is evening out, through the repetition of similar cycles, growing less disturbing over time, but not altogether.

There are the highs, there are the lows, there are times of feeling very hostile towards people, there are times when I have patience for details, times when I don't, there are times when it seems I'm smarter than at others—and times, I regret to say, when I don't have the patience I should. And there are times when the present cycle seems worse than the last one.

This brings up the question whether my self-appreciation was accurate or simply bi-polar exaggeration. When I was working before I became disabled, I was working every day the same hours in the same office, but my production wasn't the same every day. Far from it. There were times when I didn't want to go to the office and times when I couldn't wait to get there. And there may have been times when I worked maniacally. Now I've been disabled fourteen years, and there are days when I get things done around the house and days when it's very hard. And there are certainly times when I look better than I do at others—and it isn't my imagination.

In fact, one difficulty with writing about manic depression that didn't come to me so strongly in my first book, when I was writing about alcoholism is this: the answer I was given to alcoholism was essentially the Twelve Steps (I may get a little into that later, but only as much as may be necessary for this book)—and the fellowship—of Alcoholics Anonymous, what might be called a spiritual answer, and for me it has worked. The answer I was given to Manic Depression with Alcoholism was a combination of that spiritual answer and medication—or, if not medication precisely, a restoration of chemical balances in the system—and it has worked, pretty well, but it's not entirely clear what part is working, and (perhaps) what part isn't. What it would be like if I were manic depressive and not alcoholic? I can't say, because I'm both.

I have noticed lately that when I get sick—I mean, with things like flu—the illnesses don't seem to be lasting as long as they used to. I have spoken with some of my bipolar friends and they seem to have experienced the same thing. This could be the result of substituting an antidepressant for an anti-cyclothymic—a natural "evener-out" like lithium—which would probably lead to an increase in mixed-manic periods. I'm not the best judge of that. As I said, when I'm depressed I know I'm depressed, but when I'm manic I don't know I'm manic. It's only afterwards I realize I was. And not always then. And sometimes not till very long after.

Sometimes I feel that it's all a rotten break. I know there are a lot of people in this world that have a lot more wrong with them than I have with me. But when I'm really feeling down, I don't see how it can be worse. And when I'm really up my tendency is to forget how bad things can get. (Although when I've been up for a while I get afraid that it isn't going to last—and of course, so far, it hasn't lasted.)

When things aren't good I'm pretty sure I have more mixed-manic or angry-manic phases, but I just tell myself I have a reason to be angry, don't I? And I find that I do. I can't think how often my husband has reacted unfavorably to something I've said, and my response has been, "I have a right to my opinion."

So far as I know, I do—but it doesn't always seem to avoid confrontation, and my husband, given a choice, will avoid confrontation. And then, on the other hand, when he wants to fight something "on principle" (like the fact the borough where we live is charging us to bring the sidewalks they laid up to ADA standards for wheelchairs), I don't want him to "make trouble."

It all makes very good sense to me, but not always to him. Maybe it's a difference between men and women, men being more willing to fight for abstract principle (the *borough* is levying a differential tax in kind on senior citizens and the disabled in order to pay for a *federal* law intended to benefit the disabled—the ADA); maybe the differences are my manic depression coming out. I don't know, nor does he.

My own treatment for Bipolar Disorder, since 1972, has, as I say, been Lithium therapy. But there are other treatments, with other drugs, and these are becoming more popular—and other drugs are sometimes used to supplement lithium. We look at difficulties in finding other drugs or treatments for manic depression, a subject that could easily be taken as the occasion for very black humor. My condition as a manic depressive who is also alcoholic means these drugs are, as the doctors say, "contraindicated" in my case. In any case, the older lithium alternatives are mostly either Thorazine (with its "shuffle") or very close to it. As I said, no, thank you.

Fundamentally—I'm repeating myself, but it's very important to me—the only medicine I have taken for my manic depressive /bipolar condition is Lithium carbonate. (Every once in a while, recently, a doctor has suggested a quarter-tablet of Seroquel at bedtime, which is supposed to aid in sleep, I think.) The doctor who initiated my manic-depression treatment told me lithium was the only medicine I would ever need—but that, since I am a recovered alcoholic, I must also never drink again. He told me if I didn't take the lithium and go to A. A. I might drink, and if I drank I would have so much serious remorse I might be inclined to take my life.

So I have followed what he told me to the letter. I have not had a drink—right now it has been forty-seven years, as I say—and I have always taken the lithium. I don't want to drink and I don't want to try to take my life. I have some friends who are bipolar and who have taken other medicines. I don't think their recovery has been smooth. And I had three wonderful friends who were bipolar and who stopped taking lithium and killed themselves. They stopped taking it because of its effect on lovemaking, which severely depressed them. But when they stopped taking it, they got so depressed they killed themselves.

You see, lithium was only finally cleared (or "re-cleared") for U.S. usage in late 1970 and I began my lithium therapy in mid-1972, and I was young then (so I'm still around now), and right now, so far as I know, I've been on lithium longer than anyone else around—and besides that I'm an alcoholic (though sober for forty-seven years—since October 5, 1970)—and it's hard to establish standards for you when you're pretty much one of a kind, at least at the edges.

My original lithium dosage was 900 mg a day. That was in 1972. In 2008 it was cut (when Hershey Medical Center re-determined what they thought was a toxic lithium level—actually my sense was, they didn't like lithium much anyway). For a brief while after my dosage was cut, I was allowed to take 800 mg a day (well, 750, 750, and 900, because it comes in multiples of 150) and although not as comfortable as I was on 900 I was a lot better than I was on 600 or 675. (Right now I'm on 600.)

And my family notices the difference and they see the higher dosage as much more therapeutic. But then my lithium levels rose to 1.4 and I was put back to 600—and then eventually to 600 one day, 450 the next, for a while—too long by my reactions—and my family's. I'm allowed to go up to 600 a day when things are bad, but not for very long—then it's back to the 600-450-600-450, or even (sometimes) only 450 a day.

In short, I can say (even with these recent variations), my life began anew thanks to lithium carbonate and a very knowledgeable doctor. I have taken lithium virtually every day of my life since that time and although my weeks and months are sometimes rocky I was not in a day clinic. Nevertheless, life for me is still difficult. I have moderate to strong depressions and moderate to strong highs. And the lower the lithium dosage, the stronger they get.

I understand that lithium carbonate had some difficult times. Better times in Europe than here. I understand that lithium may still be improving in usage in this country (though just about every week I hear of someone who has switched off it). I hope that it is improving in usage. It's very inexpensive. And I have not had any serious side effects from taking lithium carbonate, although there was the time when my lithium levels rose briefly to 1.4 and I had tremors and Parkinsonian symptoms. My own belief is that the symptoms came from mixing lithium and the substitutes they tried to give me because my lithium levels were rising—something about the substitutes encouraging lithium retention. But I don't know that. I could be quite wrong.

Friends, by the way, are harder for me to deal with than is my family. People have a hard time with my ups and downs, and what they interpret as yelling or as criticisms. So I go through periods where the phone seldom rings, and I watch a lot of television. My cousins on the other hand are very tolerant. They know me; they understand me; and they love me. They don't see me very often so perhaps my temperament is easier for them to put up with.

I'm thinking right now of other bipolar people I've known, especially among alcoholics—it seems particularly common among women (at least in my experience), but there are cases among men too—and sometimes the bipolar men are married to the bipolar women. They take different medicines but they seem to have one thing in common—unhappiness. Well, not uniformly—they have moments when they do seem happy, in a kind of special and limited way. One friend raises special cats [Blue Point Siamese] and one has a farmette with a horse and a donkey—apparently animals help a great deal. I know I would have been much less well off without my German Shepherd Loki, who had to be put down in April two years ago. Of course, we had German shepherd dogs when I was growing up back in Prospectville.

Things from our early life stick with us—and what has stuck with me particularly is the triggered manic depressive condition (not any particular individual episodes)—triggered, I think, [1] by my mother's beating me in my childhood (my father never beat me but I remember his spanking me when I—not knowing what I was saying—used the n-word because a boy in my class had used it) and [2] by my father's death when I was twelve and Teddy was ten.

When our father died (I say "our"—after all he was Teddy's father too), my mother said it was God's fault and we weren't going to have anything to do with God any more—and she also cut every tie that she could to our father's family—she was convinced his middle-class German family wanted nothing to do with an Irish woman from the wrong side of the tracks.

That also was traumatic, and—I suppose—a kind of abuse. I had enough of the triggers to set the whole psychosis in motion—and of course, once in motion, it went on—and on. So let's begin my story, beginning in the middle. And as I tell the story, remember that one question whose answer I haven't settled is this: does my life seem a series of ups and downs because, in some sense, it really was, or because I'm a manic depressive? To put it another way, did the "highs" happen because I was high on the upswing and that's when I could, you might say, accept the highs?

It's a different version of the chicken and the egg—in effect, do we call it an egg because it comes out of the chicken (which is a bird), or do we call it a chicken (which is a bird) because it comes out of the egg? Do I have ups and downs because I'm manic depressive, or am I manic depressive because I have ups and downs?

The answer is, I believe, that having ups and downs makes me bipolar (bipolar-I or bipolar-II) or even manic-depressive (if that's different from bipolar-I as I believe it is): but it doesn't necessarily make me manic-depressive. (It may even, mildly, make me "cyclo-thymic."). But I am manic depressive, and being manic depressive, I surely have ups and downs—and they may, in a sense, intermingle, the so-called mixed state. (This, as I keep saying, is the distinguishing characteristic of the manic-depressive—there isn't just a simple cycling from up to down to up to down But the term "bi-polar" seems to suggest that the only states of importance are at the two poles—the "up" manic and the "down" depressive—and they're equally important. That's not true even for "bi-polar-I" or "-II.")

HARDSHIP FINDING BIPOLAR DRUGS

The last fifty years have seen major advances in drugs to treat (clinical) depression. There are tricyclic antidepressants, and more lately, a generation of heterocyclic antidepressants. There have also been favorable results reported with MAOIs (monoamine oxidase inhibitors). The (second generation) heterocyclics include bupropion and fluoxetine. Tricyclics include imipramine, amitryptiline, and nortryptiline—three with both "activating" and "sedating" results that may make them more suitable for bipolar patients than are the antidepressants that may simply induce hypomania or mania. But generally tricyclic antidepressants are at best of unproven value for bipolar patients. They raise the mood when you're depressed. But they're likely to raise the mood even when you're manic.

The MAOIs include Isocarboxazid, Phenelzine, Selegiline, and Tranylcypromine. Even if I were to give you their brand-names, I doubt you would have heard much about them. I haven't. The original tricyclic was imipramine, very much like chlorpromazine, the original antipsychotic, better known under its trade-name Thorazine. This was developed, or at least tested, as a way of putting insect swarms into artificial hibernation for their short lives (in other words, an insecticide).

Sure, I tell myself, I'm really anxious to dose myself with bug-spray. And besides the bug-spray factor, imipramine and its relatives are related to benzodiazepines like Valium and Librium, which are essentially alcohol in a pill for any alcoholic, so I'm not about to take imipramine. And in one test, two-thirds of bi-polar I patients taking imipramine showed manic episodes—not good.

Bupropion (that always looks like I'm misspelling it) is among the heterocyclic antidepressants (antidepressants with other than three cycles—which would be tricyclic): it is, in fact, monocyclic. But its toxic level depends on individual chemistry—I know my body chemistry is idiosyncratic, being both manic depressive and alcoholic—and having thyroid problems as well—and the result of buprorion toxicity is serious seizures. No thanks.

One drug tried for bipolar disorder is carbamazepine, also closely related to Thorazine, though the symptoms of use are not defined as a shuffle. They are however defined as tremors, dulled perception, unsteadiness and slowed walking (sounds something like a shuffle to me). Furthermore, using carbamazepine and lithium together may increase the risk of what are called neurotoxic side effects. Also, the drug may change thyroid functioning, and the changes have not been fully predictable. Again, no thanks.

All these seem to me to be treating the symptoms as much as—or more than—the condition. They deal with racing thoughts by inhibiting thoughts of any kind. They deal with the tendency to run around at full speed by making it impossible to move faster than a slow shuffle. But, as I understand it, lithium in some way attacks the underlying condition. Of course, I know just about as much about how lithium works as I do about how aspirin works. But then—I'm not sure very many people know *how* aspirin works—but it does.

HOW LITHIUM WORKS? AND OTHERS DON'T?

Still, I think it's worthwhile to try to get some idea how lithium works. Unfortunately, the specific biochemical mechanism of lithium action in stabilizing mood is unknown. When taken, lithium is widely distributed in the central nervous system and interacts with a number of neurotransmitters and receptors, for example decreasing norepinephrine release and increasing serotonin synthesis. Unlike many psychoactive drugs, Lithium typically produces no obvious psychotropic effects (such as euphoria) in normal individuals at therapeutic dose levels. Lithium may increase the release of serotonin by neurons in the brain

In the last ten years or so, two other possible area for lithium action have been suggested. It was proposed in 2007 that lithium may interact with nitric oxide (NO) signaling pathways in the central nervous system, which play a crucial role in neural plasticity. Also, Lithium possesses neuroprotective properties: it interrupts the system of programmed cell death (apoptosis) and increases cell longevity: this suggests that manic depression or bi-polar disorder comes from a system programming error.

(After conversation with the mathematician in my life, I can't help wondering if this is connected with bi-polar shift in the chaotic ordering of matter that chaos theory gives us. I'm not exactly sure what that would mean and how it would work out, but I give it for what it's worth.) Other treatments for bi-polar disorder include thyroid adjustments with *predictable* results (sometimes through levothyroxin, which I take in any case), and have included artificial light stimulus and sleep deprivation—neither with very good results, and Shock Treatments ("Electro-Convulsive Therapy"), to which I was subjected back in the day long before it was (I am told) refined to the point where it only causes partial (not virtually complete) "temporary" loss of memory. The fact that manic depression has been treated with anticonvulsants (reducing convulsions) and ECT (adding convulsions) suggests to me some uncertainties in treatment—but then, it's only *my* mind.

One question debated over the past thirty or forty years has been the connection between calcium levels and "manic depression"—specifically CSF (cerebro-spinal fluid) concentrations of calcium. This is one of the areas where I wish more work had been done (I seem to have stronger calcium in my bones than most women my age). A couple of others occur to me after again looking over the textbook. One is the "histamine transport system" in the brain. (p. 474).

Clearly, histamine interacts with mood-altering drugs—that's an experiential finding. For me at least one common anti-histamine, supposed to be sleep-inducing, is quite the opposite. Another area I'm curious about is the "seritonin transport system" (p. 475), where there seem to me—but I'm not an expert—to be significant connections between seritonin action in alcoholics—of my type at least—and seritonin action in manic-depressive (bipolar) patients—of my type at least (see the discussion in Jared Lobdell, *This Strange Illness: Alcoholism and Bill W.*, Aldine 2004). Does this mean medication is necessary? Could there be another way (as in A. A.)?

Sometimes, by the way, my mind overlooks things. I have recently been re-reading parts of the monumental Goodwin-Jamison 1990 textbook on *Manic-Depressive Illness*, and I've come across a couple of passages that I simply don't remember from 'way back then. I particularly noted one on pages 674-675. The authors tell us that lithium does not generally interfere with alcohol-induced highs. Some patients, on the other hand, drink less alcohol on lithium, particularly if their drinking had been strongly linked to mood extremes. Lithium has been reported to interfere with cocaine- and amphetamine-induced highs.

Evidently not all bi-polar patients have become sober or "clean and sober"—but perhaps they're not alcoholics (or addicts). One cannot be entirely sure, of course. Probably those bipolar patients for whom lithium and alcohol had reinforcing effects and those for whom they had opposite effects were alcoholics and non-alcoholics, or in mania rather than depression (four possibilities for two effects).

On p. 687 we find a brief discussion of men and women on lithium. For men, manic episodes on lithium decreased more than depressive episodes, but for women the effects were equal for the two types of episodes. I wonder if the greater reduction in male mania has anything to do with the fact that men find greater reduction in sexual appetite with lithium than women do—which explains (on anecdotal evidence, at least) their greater reluctance to continue on lithium therapy. And their (anecdotally) higher suicide rate.

I think perhaps this is the place to look again at that part of my story where I began my lithium treatment. After a few days in the padded cell I was allowed to wear real clothes and my meals were upstairs. Eventually I was allowed down the huge staircase to the dining room and after all I'd been through the dining room was like a palace and I could eat anything I wanted and even have seconds. They began to introduce the lithium carbonate and I did not do well. I had tremendous tremors and it was nothing for me to take a spoonful of cereal and the tremor would be so great the cereal wound up thrown across the room. I can still see that and the table I was sitting at.

Then, one day, the nurse came up to me with a little plate of crackers covered with peanut butter. There were about half a dozen crackers on the plate—no maybe four or five. I asked what they were for and I was told just to eat the crackers: the doctor had ordered them. After a week or two my tremors were gone and with just a few minor exceptions they have not returned. That was a little more than forty years ago. No, as I say in my story, I don't think the peanut butter had a physical therapeutic effect itself—unless somehow the peanut butter reduced the tremors not only psychologically (it's a "comfort food") but physiologically—but I do think it must have been necessary to get the lithium into me rather than jerked onto the wall or the floor. It's a good thing I loved peanut butter (And I still do).

HEREDITARY "MANIC DEPRESSION"?

One (more than) possibility for manic depression and its origins in any particular depressive, is that it is likely to be hereditary. There should be manic depressives back through history, long before there were medicines to treat it. King Alfred of England (Wessex) r. 871-899, is clearly one of the historical bipolar sufferers I spoke of before—"bipolars" or manic depressives.

John Adams and Meriwether Lewis are two in the early days of our Republic. Lewis committed suicide (I believe—though some historians have argued for murder in revenge for previous behavior); John Adams seems to have come to a resolution of his bipolar troubles sometime between the 1800 election and the day during the War of 1812 when Benjamin Rush convinced him to write to Jefferson. (I invite an historian of the Early American Republic to look into this.) Let's try a list of sufferers from bipolar disorder in history, and see where it can lead us.

Since the British Monarchy is hereditary, we might expect Alfred's descendants on the British throne to demonstrate bipolar characteristics. From his son Edward the Elder through his great-grandson Ethelred the Unready, through his son Edward Confessor, this seems to hold, though that's only a surface impression for now. Ethelred's son Edmund left a daughter who married into the Scots Royal family— and it the Scottish monarchy as well as the English shows the bipolar characteristics through the Middle Ages and the Stuart Kings (from whom the British line after 1603 descends, though attenuated).

Among Medieval English kings, Richard II (r. 1377-1399), son of the Black Prince (also arguably Bipolar/Manic Depressive) stands out, who inconsolably burned down the special palace he built for his Queen, when she died.

Other notable persons suspected of bipolar disorder (besides writers and artists mentioned by Kay Redfield Jamison) include Abraham Lincoln and Sir Winston Churchill (and his cousin Lady Diana, Princess of Wales). It has been suggested that Ulysses Grant may have been bipolar. (Napoleon, I am told, has also been suggested as bipolar, but sometimes it seems like it's a parlor game or a version of a Jeopardy category, "Possible Famous 'Bipolars' in History.")

Sir Winston may have self-medicated with brandy and champagne. Grant's drinking may have been self-medication. The point is, there is no record of recovery by most of these, because—of course—you cannot talk much about recovery from an illness until you have defined or diagnosed—or at least discovered there is—this illness. That doesn't mean people haven't fought through it over the ages.

QUESTION 3: VISION? DREAM? VR? CURE WITHIN?

When under Dr. Zarate, I came out of the angry manic state (which had swiftly followed the depressed state) in a way familiar to me now from William James's *The Varieties of Religious Experience*—a book recommended for alcoholics in A. A. ever since Bill W. began reading it back in 1934. And there was something else now familiar to me from William James and from Bill W.

For many years previous to 1970, at least ten, I had been a nightmare sleeper five or six nights a week. I had horrible dreams of rodents and reptiles and fences with spikes on them, and most nights I woke up screaming. The night my drinking ended, however, I didn't have a nightmare—I had what I now think of as my white dream. In the dream there was a large window with no curtains and glistering white sunlight poured in that window almost as white as diamonds. I had never had a dream like that before, and I just dismissed it—I didn't even mention it to my sponsor (when I got a sponsor) for five or six months. I was glad the horrible nightmares had gone—they've never come back—but I really didn't think much about the dream itself.

This may be fanciful, but one can read about historical characters who were clearly bipolar, and find something like a conversion experience going on (in the William James sense). The story of King Alfred at Athelney, with what happened before and after, is certainly open to that interpretation. If we look through history at sufferers from bipolar disorder (which was mostly in the past called manic depression, if anything at all), we find that, being no recognized disease, there was no treatment. But occasionally some hints are given in discussions of religious conversion. It is true many of these deal with what must have been Secondary Depressive Alcoholism; a few deal with depression (presumably clinical depression).

I've wondered often if it's reasonable to discuss a dream as a treatment for alcoholism or for bipolar disorder. And yet... and yet...

Recent research on what Dr. Jung called "Big Dreams"—which can also include both hypnogogic and hypnopompic visual experiences ("dreams" on the edge between sleeping and waking, or between waking and sleeping)—can actually alter the pattern of action in the brain, either by altering the relative importance of different neurotransmitters, or by altering the pace of transmission, or by altering the transmission paths.

Now in my case, I believe that, because I had begun the alteration of my brain by drinking alcoholically to allay my "bipolar disorder" (or, as I thought of it then, my "manic depression"), the brain-altering effect of my white-light dream was felt in my alcoholic answer to my bipolar problem, and not directly in the bipolar condition itself. On the other hand, if a manic depressive has not found a self-remedy in drinking, maybe his dream changed the brain chemistry in a way that directly spoke to his bipolar condition. I already noted there may be a connection between serotonin transport problems in alcoholism and bipolar conditions.

So I think it's time to look at the brain effects of visions, and at the brain effects of the "Big Dreams" and at the brain effects of virtual reality (V.R.), and how these may tie in with the alleviation or cure or "treatment" of manic depression. I know that Dr. Jung made a distinction between visions (which come when one is partly awake) and dreams (which come when one is asleep): in fact he distinguished between waking/sleeping visions and sleeping/waking visions, though I don't know if the difference was significant. Some people think visions are somehow more "real" than dreams.

But in my mind, and from my experience, both seem to lead to changes in the mind, presumably in the brain. The recent book on *Big Dreams*, by Kelly Bulkeley, notes that many dream-analysts—the "materialists"—write (and talk) as though dreams and visions come from existing conditions of the brain. I suppose that may be true—but what is important, to me, is that the dreams or visions (as with Henry Alline, as with a number of alcoholics caught up in William James's *Varieties of Religious Experience*, and as with me), seem to have created changes in patterns of thought—that is, created changes in some part of brain structure, or at least in neurotransmission.

This is going to get us into what I believe is called CSR—the cognitive science of religion. As I understand it, the "scientists" or "materialists" claim that, unless there's an actual physical change in our systems, including our brain-systems, there has been no "cure" (by that means). On the other hand, there are those who claim there is some kind of "cure" that "seems to violate the basic premise of modern medicine, by ignoring the actual physiological workings of the body and naively accepting the allegedly healing effects of thoughts, prayers and dreams" *(Big Dreams,* p. 248)—but "real scientific evidence is increasingly pointing to a dynamic interplay between mind and body." I think this tends to get mixed up after a while with the so-called *placebo* effect, by which something works if you think it's going to work. My own experience (and the effect of dreams—or visions) is that there's a kind of kernel, an irreducible area where there is physiological change apparently external to the system.

I suppose this could fit in with what we might call "spiritual drug therapy"—I'm thinking back to alcoholism and to experiments with LSD-25, not as a direct curative (whatever that would be in this case), but as a way to bring about new patterns of thought in which (like some kind of religious or spiritual experience) the patient could be further schooled or trained.

The founder of Alcoholics Anonymous, Bill W., working with Dr. Hoffer, thought this a promising area for research until Timothy Leary and others rather spoiled things. That was a long while before my own experience in A. A. The *Big Dreams* book calls attention to the work of clinical psychotherapist James W. Jones, and the fact that therapeutic approaches like hypnosis, mental imagery, biofeedback, and meditation argue effectively for an up-and-down process where the brain affects the mind and *the mind affects the brain*—and an outside force (a dream?) can affect the mind and thus the brain, or affect the brain directly.

There is a curious example in *The Varieties of Religious Experience* where a bright-light dream or vision—a bright-light experience, in any case—was experienced, apparently objectively, not only by the subject, but by others with him (in the story of "The Apostle to the Lost").

Of course it could be some kind of mass hallucination—but the subject remained sober the rest of his life, and came to be known as the "Apostle of the Lost." My vote is for the two-way influence. And that fits in with my experience in the retraining of my mind (and neural connections) in Alcoholics Anonymous.

It's my belief (and I'm viewing the whole thing partly from inside) that the effect of prayer, for example, is not simply to be explained as a kind of *placebo* effect. I mean, I don't think prayer works only because I think it's going to work—though I suppose that could explain it.

There could be a physiological shift simply as a result of my belief there's going to be—but that isn't what is usually meant by the *placebo* effect. I know that I have been prayed for, without much belief on my part that it was going to work—and then it did. And I have recently experienced a case where a pastor prayed for a third person to cease a course of behavior that was driving me to distraction—and she did. (He has no personal contact with the third person—doesn't know her name.)

The process of prayer does sometimes seem to work in and of itself (though some would simply put it down to coincidence). And there are the times—not frequent—when I'm aware the process isn't working—and then it does. If we follow *Big Dreams* (and Dr. Jung) in believing that the origins of religion are in dreams and visions, and if we are believers, then I guess we have to accept cures by prayer, cures by bright-light dream—and I'm wondering if folk-medicine and acupuncture may not fit in here. I'm not going to stop taking my medicine—and I'm not going to stop praying either—and I'm not going to deny mind-cure or deny the *physical* effect of dreams or visions.

But let's look briefly at these other areas. What is the *placebo* effect and can this be it? What physically does a dream or vision do, and is this a right question to be asking?

What about "folk-remedy" experience and such matters as acupuncture—or shamanistic or "Native American" or Tibetan experience?

What about Christian Science and Spiritual Science? What about Mind-Healing? What about what is generally called "Faith-healing?"

I don't know the answers, of course, but for what it's worth, I can testify to my belief—experiential as well as theological—that there's something beyond "mere *placebo*" with all of these. And then there's what happened to me when I was first sober in the Philadelphia area in late 1971/early 1972. I was prayed for then by people in A. A., of course, but I had a consciousness somehow that I was very greatly prayed for, prayers beyond prayers, so to speak.

My present married name is the same as that of my husband's mother, who was sober from 1947 to her death in Philadelphia in early 1972. When I was feeling the impact of those prayers beyond prayers, she was being very greatly prayed for, there in Philadelphia and beyond, and her name then was the same as mine now—and "now" (I am taught) is when God works. Not sure that's theologically sound—but once again, it's experientially true, in my experience—though it took me forty years to come up with the explanation. (Her middle name, even, was the same as mine.) Or maybe it's all imagination? Or subjective reality?

In her book *The Cure Within* (New York 2008), Anne Harrington wrote of the Beatles and Transcendental Meditation and meditation as the next thing to try after psychedelic drugs (p. 209). Now there's no doubt that meditation can help physically—with "nerves," let us say. The founder of Alcoholics Anonymous, Bill W., used a spiritual regimen of walking, breathing in step, and using a prayer as a kind of mantra, in step with the breathing and walking—and, ideally, his heart-rate.

Research by Mathieu Ricard and Jean-François Revel and others in the past twenty years has suggested very strong gamma brain waves from meditators experienced in (Tibetan and similar) meditation techniques. (pp. 241-242). Once again, I don't know how this works, or the degree to which it does, but I know from my A. A. experience that something is working here, and what I've read from William James on fits in. I'll go on praying and meditating. Of course, I'd go on doing that even if odds were the only effect is the *placebo* effect—but that's not it.

Obviously we cannot solve this problem here, or even do anything more than point out there's a dimension to "cure" here, or even amelioration that may go far beyond what medication can bring about. Every once in a while I hear someone at an A. A. meeting slip and say "prayer and medication." But then, the meditation is an alternative medication.

Laughter is the best medicine? No, it is a medicine, but devotions may be better. Certainly, until we know the fundamental relationship of mind and matter, we aren't going to know best what to do with our minds—or with material medicines. And what is the relationship between what we see and what is? I've made it to the age of seventy-six, forty-seven years sober, forty-five on Lithium as a manic depressive, and I still don't know the relationship. But I've made it to this point.

Recent work with virtual reality seems to suggest questions along the same lines. So did some of the early experiments with Lysergic Acid Diethylamide-25. I suspect acupuncture could likewise speak to the body-mind connection. I know I gave up smoking through acupuncture—I was the only one of six (all alcoholics) in our group to do so successfully—and I was the only "manic depressive."

I know from talking to my son about his experience that immersion in Virtual Reality can lead shortly to obvious physical effects. Obviously "spiritual healing" (if it's real) speaks to the same point. As we were finishing this section of the book (I have to dictate to my husband because my other ailments have conspired to make typing impossible and writing mostly impossible), there was an article in *TIME* Magazine (September 5, 2016) on virtual reality as a treatment for chronic pain:

"As VR technology gets better, cheaper and more accessible—thanks in part to consumer-friendly headsets like the Oculus Rift ... a small but growing number of scientists and entrepreneurs are using it to treat medical conditions, including PTSD and chronic pain" (p. 17).

The VR recreation of battle scenarios (for PTSD) is essentially a more immersive version of "exposure therapy" in which people talk about traumatic events in order to process them, and this will (apparently) work for those who cannot "emotionally engage" with their imaginations.

Confronting the past is part of the working of Alcoholics Anonymous; over the years I have concluded that the process can be immeasurably helped (in those who have them) by "white-light" dreams. I suspect the VR process may feed into that. In any case—in all these cases—what we are doing is having our thought-processes re-directed.

Certainly I see (in me) connections between the re-direction of recovery from alcoholism and the re-direction of living with manic depression. And it isn't just the direction and pattern of thought: it's also the speed. The whole business of racing thoughts in my bipolar life ties in with my alcoholic experiences—in fact, it's hard to tell whether symptoms are those of alcoholism or manic depression. They have a number of characteristics in common.

We'll come to this in the next section. What is the relationship between Manic Depression and Alcoholism?

QUESTION 4: BIPOLAR/ALCOHOLIC LINKS?

In a way, this book has some of its origins in a remark by Dr. William Duncan Silkworth (1872-1951), quoted in *Alcoholics Anonymous* (1939, fourth edition, New York: 2001, p. xxx), the "Big Book" of the fellowship of Alcoholics Anonymous (A. A.): "There is the manic-depressive type [of alcoholic], who is, perhaps, the least understood by his friends, and about whom a whole chapter could be written." But this not that Chapter—nor is that chapter in this book.

As noted, I am an alcoholic (sober in A. A. since October 5, 1970) diagnosed as manic depressive (now called bipolar) and on lithium carbonate treatment since July 1972. I believe I have been on lithium treatment longer than any other person alive (at least in the United States), and if not, I'm close.

We'll get into that pretty much right away. But, before we do, let me repeat something of what we've just said. I asked why my dream/vision/cure (whatever we call it) was for alcoholism, but others were apparently for manic depression. An obvious answer was that those "manic depressives" didn't drink alcoholically, so couldn't be cured of alcoholic drinking. I did and could be—particularly since my alcoholism came from my bipolar condition.

Indeed it may be said my alcoholism was a kind of answer to it. Of course, if alcoholic drinking is the palliative to manic depression, or even the answer, and if all of a sudden my alcoholic drinking is cured, then I need another treatment for my manic depression. (Has the benefit of the "white-dream" been, so to speak, used up on the alcoholism?) That's one relationship between Manic Depression and Alcoholism

Is there more than one relationship? Or, to put it better, what are the strands of parts of a complex interrelationship—beginning at some point before we get to the whole business of the various neuro-transmitters and the high percentage of manic depressives also alcoholic, and *vice versa*. Time for a box—on alcoholism.

FIFTH BOX—CHARACTERISTICS OF "ALCOHOLICS"
"An alcoholic is an egomaniac with an inferiority complex."

EGOMANIAC
Insomnia/less need for sleep
Exaggerated inappropriate happiness
Inappropriate grandiosity/Exaggerated self-esteem
Unrealistic beliefs about one's own powers
More energy than normal
Exaggerated talkativeness
Racing thoughts
Hyper-sexuality

INFERIORITY COMPLEX
Exaggerated sadness/fearfulness
No ability to enjoy things
No desire to be with family or friends
Withdrawal/isolation
No motivation to do things one used to enjoy
Tiredness/low energy
Poor performance at school or work
Wishing one were dead
Thoughts of suicide/even attempts at suicide

This is a matter of "affect." Now "affect" was one of the words that used to puzzle me, and I'm not sure I have it right after all these years. Nevertheless, here's a first attempt at definition. Affect is the experience of feeling or emotion, and is one of the three "a-b-c" domains of modern psychology—affect, behavior, and cognition. Affective states are what are called psycho-physiological (that is, both psychological and physiological) and vary according to valence, arousal, and motivational intensity.

"Valence" is another word I find puzzling, and I'm not sure it's necessary, but it's the way psychologists talk. *Valence*, as used in psychology, especially in discussing emotions, means the intrinsic attractiveness (positive valence) or unattractiveness (negative valence) of an event, object, or situation. The term is also used to categorize specific emotions. For example, the emotions popularly referred to as "negative," such as anger and fear, have "negative valence". Joy has "positive valence." The old idea was that the degree of valence helped determine motivational intensity and that high motivational intensity broadened cognitive scope—if you got really emotionally involved in something you could understand it better—in psychological terms, that affect was positively related to cognition. But it is now believed, for the second part at least, that the opposite is true. Well, maybe—and for some of us, maybe not. We'll come back to that, too.

MY OWN STATE—THINGS I DIDN'T LEARN FROM BOOKS

As I said, when I was diagnosed—forty-five years ago—my "craziness" was called manic depressive psychosis. Now it's called bi-polar disorder—bipolar-I. For me, whatever it's called, it's been very difficult through the years—particularly because I have these extreme mood swings, and though when I'm down I know I'm down, when I'm up I don't think I'm up—and certainly not manic.

My brother was diagnosed as manic depressive, just as I was, and was prescribed Lithium carbonate medication to take, pretty much just as I was. He refused to take it. The result? While my life has been up and down, I believe my brother's was more up and down. He died at fifty-one of lung cancer—refusing to stop smoking—and by that time he had been divorced (and he died trying to reach his former wife on the phone—there's a kind of up-and-down I hope I never reach).

I only know of one other member of my family with this condition and that was one of my mother's brothers, my Uncle Rich, who was in the Second World War and was injured and was sent back to the States to be in a psychiatric hospital. He was in the VA Hospital a couple of times after that. He was an extremely nice man and I loved him a lot. I don't know of any cousins who are bi-polar.

Uncle Rich had no children. So my brother and I and Uncle Rich are the only ones I can be sure of. Fortunately there was a change in treatment for manic depression after my Uncle Rich was hospitalized: Uncle Rich was in Framingham Hospital in Massachusetts, treated with iced sheets and also treated by being tied up. But that was long ago when there were bomb shelters at Framingham.

The hospitalization under Dr. Carlos A. Zarate, Sr., that I have written about was my last until a couple of years ago when the local medical center reduced the amount of lithium they would let their patients take—or, to be exact, they lowered the permissible level of lithium in the blood before they diagnosed borderline lithium toxicity—so I went from 900 to 600 mg daily (permissible lithium level reduced from 1.4 to 1.1). Guess what? I've been hospitalized twice since my dosage was reduced—though very brief hospitalizations, only a few days at a time, for observation.

Before the lithium, my depressions and my highs were both less moderate, though the highs seem not to have been quite as high as others I have read about. The highs are marked by moving fast, a louder voice, freedom from restraint with money, and more than average desires for sex. My family of course now recognizes all of my highs and lows and for the most part my family members are tolerant. They know I have a serious illness and the lithium does wonders but it doesn't take the illness away. (Every once in a while I talk to another manic depressive who uses something else, not lithium, and I wonder if I ought to switch—and I don't know if that's the voice of reason or of my disease.)

All this questioning of dosage and recounting of manic episodes brings us (perhaps brings us back) to the question of the inter-relationship of manic depression and alcoholism and to a vignette in my history that ought to be included here as well as further on. The manic episodes are not easily distinguishable from alcoholic highs, in my experience or (so far as I know) that of others.

Talking loud and fast, throwing money around like a drunken (!) sailor, thinking you see relationships between everything and everything else that disappear when you're sober—is this manic? Or drunk? And here's the vignette. Dr. Carlos Zarate telling me in 1972 that I would need to take lithium for my manic depression and A. A. for my alcoholism. So let's perhaps talk a little more about the meeting of manic depression and alcoholism. (My grandson's girlfriend helped me set up a weblog ("blog") on this—"Alcoholic-Bipolar-Conversation" [A-B-C] and I'm learning how to use it so we can carry on this discussion.)

MEETING OF MANIC DEPRESSION
AND ALCOHOLISM

Over the years, as my account makes clear, I've learned enough to know that there is a connection—perhaps more than one connection—between the two diseases. (Actually, Dr. Kay Redfield Jamison has estimated that 60 percent of manic depressives are alcoholic drinkers.) I think I understand enough about both diseases, even from my own experience, not to mention what I have read, to know that both have to do with neurotransmission, that they have some characteristics in common, and that there is a kind of alcoholism that very often is connected to manic depression. A recent book (well, 2004) calls it Secondary Depressive Alcoholism—secondary because the alcoholism often develops from the depressive condition.

I asked more than one physician why I didn't know I was a manic depressive until 1972 (even with being in mental hospitals), and they told me that alcoholism and alcohol masked the illness. (There was one doctor in New Jersey who told me before Dr. Zarate, but he—I said to myself, and to my husband—didn't know what he was talking about. They tell me—alcoholics tell me—that alcoholism is the only disease that tells you that you don't have it. Wrong! I know another—and I have it, and I'm talking about it now)

When I was sober eleven months I went to that doctor in New Jersey who diagnosed me as manic depressive and I couldn't accept it—I told him I was just having trouble with my early sobriety; I was recovering from alcoholism; I was in the early stages of recovery—and I certainly didn't appreciate his diagnosis. He told me I had to take lithium every day. My husband told me I had to take it. The tremors were horrible—other medicine was added—the tremors were still horrible—and I finally left the hospital "a.m.a"—against medical advice. But before I left he told me it would get worse. I had no intention of letting it get worse—but it got worse.

What was important here was my complete denial of anything but alcoholism. But the situation did get worse, and eventually I couldn't continue to deny it. The other thing of course had been the tremors which I got from the lithium the way he was administering it to me, which I hated (no peanut butter from him). Tremors are very unpleasant, of course, but the most important thing was, that, the first time around, I absolutely and totally disbelieved the doctor who told me I was manic depressive and that it would get worse, though he was right on both.

I was never diagnosed as a manic depressive until that time in New Jersey. I was 28, and I had been hospitalized six or seven times. After which I was given lithium carbonate, which I did not take then but have taken ever since. My brother had the same diagnosis at the same time but I took my medicine and he didn't. We were both members of A. A. at the time and his sponsor recommended he not take any medication and my sponsor recommended I take it. So I did and he didn't. As a result he had more jobs than you could shake a stick at—he couldn't hold them. I on the contrary had fewer jobs and held them pretty well.

What the New Jersey doctor didn't tell me, and Dr. Zarate didn't tell me, and I still don't know, is why I was a manic depressive. Was it because I was beaten in early childhood? Was it because of a childhood injury? Was it because of an inherited predisposition? I still don't know. But maybe there's some chance of finding out, if we look at what (according to the doctors) this condition is.

You remember, back "in the day" it was thought that a shortage of norepinephrine in the system was linked to depressive states. In my study of alcoholism I learned that alcohol, generally thought of as a depressant, aids in boosting norepinephrine into the system, at least up to a point. (As I noted, we don't know what that point is.) Substantial reduction in dopamine transmission likewise may mark the depressive phase, though here it may not be the quantity so much as the ease of transmission that is of interest for the manic depressive. Alcohol intake seems to be positively related to dopamine transmission, in what I'm told is the relevant range, in most cases.

On the other hand, it is high acetylcholine levels that are connected with manic depressive condition and alcohol intake reduces acetylcholine levels. But of course all this only shows that alcohol intake will lessen the severity of depressive states. Is it possible that in manic states alcohol might go back to acting as a depressant? It would tie things up pretty neatly if it did, but we don't know, and I'm not at all sure how we'd find out.

But—and here is something that would work both ways, I think—the more serotonin in the manic depressive's system, the more rapid the shifts from up to down to up, the more rapid—in other words—

the cycling from pole to pole. It seems—as I learned from studying alcoholism—that alcohol blocks serotonin from acting in the system. Alcohol, by blocking serotonin, would—and does—slow down the cycling. So alcohol might be thought of as the manic depressive's self-medication for manic depression.

Certainly there is the strong correlation we mentioned between manic depression and alcoholism. It has been estimated that alcoholism (meaning here mostly what is technically called alcohol dependence) is four times as likely to occur with manic depressives [or at least bi-polar I subjects] as with the general population, twice as likely as with bi-polar II subjects, three times as likely as with clinical or major depressives. But it's "out of the frying pan, into the fire," if the manic depressive is also an alcoholic. I was. I am. But I'm an alcoholic who hasn't had a drink since October 5, 1970.

I read the stories of other manic depressives and I'm struck by how high their highs were and how low their lows were—and then, I wonder. Do I realize how high and how low because that's my experience, even though I can't put it as well into words—but their words arouse my own memories? Or is my own experience more muted, quieter—though it has never seemed muted at the time—possibly quieted by the alcoholic drinking? I don't know.

What I do know is that a manic depressive who doesn't acknowledge the seriousness of the condition—and I think "seriousness" is a mild word—is on the road to trouble if not disaster. I remember a fellow manic-depressive who used to tell me his case wasn't as bad as mine and he didn't need medicine—told me that more than a few times over the years I knew him—and in the end he put his gun in his mouth and pulled the trigger.

If your medicine—whether it is alcohol self-prescribed or, say, Seroquel doctor-prescribed—quells the cycling, slows it down and thus makes it more gradual, then it's effective for both the ups and the downs. But if drinking alcohol raises norepinephrine and dopamine levels and lowers acetylcholine levels, thus—in all three cases—acting to counter depression, wouldn't it raise highs even higher?

But, I tell myself, alcohol is generally thought of as a depressant and so far as I know, for most people, it is. Is it possible that the effect of alcohol is itself bi-polar? (I'm told that modern "chaos theory" tells us that in some useful senses, the whole world, the universe, if you like, is bi-polar. I'm not ready to go anywhere with that—yet)

I recently discovered a clue that might help us here. Stress System [Renin-Angiotensin] activity lowers alcohol consumption by having peripheral [non-central] events set into motion central processes that eventually inhibit alcohol intake. That is, stress *eventually* inhibits alcohol consumption through automatic processes meant to protect the body. This has been observed with the actions (for example) of vasopressin, oxytocin, and aldosterone on memory processes (obviously this wasn't learned in casual conversation.

It has been suggested that a bioactive peptide is activated in the Stress System by alcoholic intake (the Stress System itself being activated by alcoholic intake), then produces a stop or satiation signal at a point determined by emotional state, diet, environmental motivators, and individual predisposition, in a process parallel to—and very likely connected with—the process of memory.

Maybe alcohol, in people with certain body chemistries, stimulates when one is depressed and depresses when one is stimulated—raises the lows and lowers the highs? Maybe that's too simple (it probably is). Maybe the shift over from stimulation comes through a "satiation" or "stop" signal.

If that is true it might help explain why my memories seem mostly less vivid than those of other manic depressives—especially when I try to put them in words. But then, our everyday language is for everyday things and everyday conditions, and for heightened conditions we need heightened language—which I'm not really capable of.

And if I'm really depressed, then I don't communicate well at all: neither heightened language nor everyday language can communicate the depths. Suicide attempts communicate the depths. I have trouble putting my down places and down phases into words—the experiences are too definite, too sharp, too nasty, and too full, and the words are too vague, too cloudy, too indefinite, and too thin. (Of course, that can also be true for heightened states, but for me, I think the difficulty is greater for the depressive ones.)

I look back over the years since my manic depression and my alcoholic drinking were both—apparently—triggered by my father's death when I was twelve and the worsening of my mother's abusive behavior then. When my father was alive there were adventures—

children always have adventures—but they were safe and I was safe. Afterwards there were still adventures, but no safety. And really there was no home. Oh, I had places to live—really nice places that I still think of with affection, and I know "you can't go home again," but my life was centered on the house in Prospectville until my father died—and then, when he died, my life really didn't have a center.

Somehow I've never been fired from a job although I've been disciplined. I am a very good worker and I think, like most manic depressives, I have a higher-than-average intelligence. My relationships with men have been more difficult than with jobs and more difficult than I would like. It seems to be very hard to live with someone who is always up and down.

Apparently I am like other bipolar people (manic depressives) in that I have always been a worker, even when depressed—though certainly not as rapidly then. From the days at my dad's greenhouses to working in the night club, to working in an office as a girl Friday, as a book-keeper (and even working around the house or in A. A., I've had a tendency to work until I dropped.

But when I was down I wasn't always so much on time—wherever I worked, I worked, and I was never a person who fell down on the job. I don't know if this is because I'm bipolar or because my parents were both very hard-working people, but when I had a job I was always working. (Perhaps I only got jobs when I was "up" and the presence of the job helped keep me "up.")

I just about always arrived on time and I remember liking what I did. But when I was "down"—as I must have been my early sober days in A. A.—I wasn't always so much on time. Early on I remember an old-timer telling me at an A. A. meeting, "Sweetie, the time has come to be on time"—so evidently at that time I wasn't.

Now this suggests that alcohol had been a mood-elevator for me, and it's time to get (as much as I can) into the chemical or biochemical or neurological relationship between manic depression and alcoholism (We'll talk a little more about that connection when we discuss the interaction of alcohol and lithium.) Now we can turn to the connected question of memory.

Are the colors of my memories—or their strength or their sharpness—dimmed by my alcoholic drinking, which came as an alcoholic's response to my manic depression? Is it coincidental that the sharpest memories—and the brightest colors—come from when my father was alive, before I was drinking? Is it significant that my memories of the incident at Salem (we come to that later on) are bright but—literally—uncolored, black and white?

REFLECTIONS (SOME ON SUICIDE)

Does my life seem to have been a series of ups and downs because, in some sense, it really was, or does it seem to have been a series of ups and downs because I'm a manic depressive? Or could it be a kind of combination—the "highs" happen because I was high on the upswing and that's when I could, you might say, accept the highs? I don't know. I generally prefer simple explanations—but which one is the simple explanation? Or is there really any simple explanation?

I think back on my early life and the brightest pictures are the greenhouses—with my father—and the country club—with my father (particularly with him diving)—and the horseback riding—with my father and mother—and the pony cart my father had for us—in short, the times and places with my father, and the things he made. The box for skates he made in Prospectville sixty-five years ago is in our garage in Elizabethtown now.

After his death there are some times bright in memory (we'll come to these) —the trip to Nantucket with my Peck & Peck wardrobe, other times with Louis and Louis's family, Nick and the plates of spaghetti and meatballs in Bethlehem, my getting into and through my airline training and some of the time I was living in Minneapolis, actually being a stewardess and on my own.

And then, later, there was my buying my Mustang for cash, being hired by Mr. G., marrying Mr. G, our getting custody of his daughters, Andrew's birth, taking Andrew places, my marriage to my third husband when my Uncle Bill sent orchids for every table for the reception.

But some of the stronger scenes in my memory (and I'll come to these too) —the more definite memories—are bad—in the woods at Salem—the Coast Guard boarding us off Maryland—the volleyballs I heard bouncing when I was in the hospital that translated to my head bouncing around the room. And then there are some lower-toned good memories—when my brother and mother and my Uncle Mike had all gotten sober, going together to AA meetings, or meeting each other there, a "family disease" becoming a family recovery. And then there are the strong panic memories—Vermont and the Delaware Turnpike and the Pennsylvania Turnpike—they're not visually as coherent, though the most panicked of all, the Salem Wood, was at least brightly lit and visually clear (though not much in the way of color), even if I was in the dark.

I think I can see a pattern. My father's death pretty much marked the onset of my bipolar shifts, and the first shift was way down to the point where my mother broke contact with my father's family and we broke contact (as far as she was concerned) with God. After that time the greatest highs, giving the most brightly-colored memories, came when I was out of the new life I'd been plunged into—the life without my father, without my father's income, without my father's family, without my father's God.

It was within the next year after my father died that my cousin got married, and I was in the wedding, aged thirteen—and I got drunk and couldn't remember what I'd done or where I'd been—and that started my career as an alcoholic drinker. I believe that, just as I had the genetic makeup that gave me a predisposition for alcoholism, so I had the genetic makeup that gave me a predisposition for manic depressive psychosis. Both of these are matters of brain chemistry. Drinking did act to cover over the manic depression, but I certainly didn't consciously drink because of the manic depression—which I didn't know I had. But we can see how it worked. Let's look back at what we said in the Prologue.

Let me ask again. Are the colors of my memories—or their strength or their sharpness—dimmed by my alcoholic drinking, which came as an alcoholic's response to my manic depression? Is it coincidental that the sharpest memories—and the brightest colors— come from when my father was alive, before I was drinking? Is it significant that my memories of the incident at Salem are bright but—literally—uncolored, black and white?

Are there likely to be serious side effects from my taking lithium carbonate for more than forty years (forty-four now)? And what would be the alternative? And after forty years of lithium therapy, how do we know what the levels should be (it probably has something to do with kidney condition)? There was a time when my lithium levels rose to 1.4, my lithium intake was reduced, and I had tremors and Parkinsonian symptoms. My own belief is that the symptoms came from mixing lithium and the substitutes they tried to give me because my lithium levels were rising—and perhaps the substitutes themselves encourage lithium retention. But I don't know that. I would like to—but there isn't very much in the way of non-anecdotal evidence. And some of the anecdotes are about me, so I don't know how representative of others they are. And they are, of course, mostly, the only anecdotes I know.

ALCOHOLISM, MANIC DEPRESSION, AND SUICIDE

In the end, the last question I have for the moment, and the one that almost certainly cannot be answered, is this: what would my bipolar life have been like without the lithium carbonate? "Supposition contrary to fact," my philosophy professor used to say, and we can't tell. But under those "counterfactual" circumstances, I suspect I would have gone back to drinking—and I would probably be dead from the drinking. That is I would be dead from the drinking if I hadn't reached that point which manic depression frequently reaches, the point of suicide—and in that case I would probably be dead by my own hand, quickly rather than slowly.

That sounds pretty melodramatic. But the private hospitals and the whole institutional system of mental health care disappeared twenty-five to thirty years ago in a frenzy of mainstreaming patients into the real world they had fled. I can remember feeling, in the words of a play I recall (or was it a song?), "Stop the world—I want to get off." That's not a useful feeling if you not only can't get off but have to get further into the world.

Even so, horrible as my depressive phases have been, dangerous as my manic (spending and sexual) phases have been, really uncomfortable as my mixed manic (or angry manic or irritable manic) phases have been (not only for me—pretty uncomfortable for my family and others around me), when I read memoirs by other manic depressives, I wonder if my alcoholic self-medication (if that's what it was) did not in fact reduce the severity of my manic depressive psychosis. (I don't think the sentence was that long when I dictated it—now that I'm reading it over, I wonder—but I'm sure the words are mine.) The problem was, if that was the case—if alcoholic self-medication reduced the severity of the psychosis—the operation (the drinking) was in a fair way to be a success, but the patient (because I was an alcoholic) was in a fair way to die.

Just as we were finishing up the first draft of this part of the book, my husband and I went up the road for coffee—and on the way we saw a whole flock (or would it be gaggle) of school buses, the old yellow school buses, waiting to pick up students after school at the school down the street from where we live. And I suddenly cheered up at the sight—and I realized, there's something still part of life from before my father's death—the old yellow school bus.

And when he was a little boy, we took my grandson Jeffrey down to the house in Prospectville, and I have pictures of him there, linking the times, though of course the house doesn't look anything like what it did then. And on my birthday one year, my husband and I drove by the old house (we had just been to visit my parents' grave at Whitemarsh Cemetery, close by), and found the building open with renovations being made, and I stood, with my husband, in my old bedroom just about half a century after my father died. You can't go home again, but it may help if the home is still there—or at least the house is. All good links with the good past are welcome—even school buses.

And it's a good thing that, being in A. A., I tell my story a couple of times a year at speakers' meetings: it's part of what we're promised in A. A.—we will not regret the past or turn our back on it. I don't know if my adventures in manic depression are fully representative of the lives and adventures of other (especially non-alcoholic) manic depressives, so I don't know whether my suggestions will be as valuable to these as they will be to the alcoholic manic-depressives like me. But I'm convinced the manic depression is the primary disease—the alcoholism is "secondary depressive"—so they should work well enough.

In Alcoholics Anonymous, we have to study our Twelve Steps and I didn't get anything out of anything some of the time when I first came in and my manic depression hadn't been fully diagnosed. We had to study those steps and I just couldn't do it and I didn't understand why it took me longer than anyone else and then my sponsor told me it could be my mood shifts. My condition still seems to slow me down when I'm down and speed me up when I'm up. I see myself as better stronger smarter than I am—and then at the other end of the pole I'm just not as smart as I was last week. And when my mind (and mood) cycles, I lose much—if not all—of what I've just learned. So, on the whole, despite some speeding up in the "up" phases, the net effect of all the shifts back and forth is losing concentration, losing consistency (of course), and losing time.

I'm not sure my other manic depressive (or bi-polar) friends in A. A. have had the same experience. Here are very brief biographies of four friends of mine in A. A. that fit with our subject here. I've disguised the names to keep anonymity.

EMMETT

First is Emmett, 53. He is a product of private schools and is in the clothing business. He had a psychiatrist for a number of years but greatly disagreed with the medications he had to take. He was a tall handsome man and the ladies liked him. He felt that the medication (lithium) greatly inhibited his romantic life, and after several years of not taking the medication, he took his own life at age 54.

AMY

Next is Amy, and Amy is a bright attractive woman who was involved in a severe auto accident and the accident left her crippled. She had to take medications for pain and for manic depression, and she was in a wheelchair. Her husband took her to Ireland (in the wheelchair). She had a wonderful family, became a mother relatively early in life and a grandmother also early on. She had frequent hospitalizations, and refused to take her medication. Her husband came home from work, found her almost unconscious, took her to the hospital: they resuscitated her. A week later he came home from work, and this time it was too late.

SUSAN

Susan was an RN and won many citations for her work in pediatric medicine. She married the man of her dreams and had two children. She continued with her nursing career and her husband continued working for the government and he traveled. She had many ups and downs and was finally diagnosed as a manic depressive and at the same time learned her husband was having an affair. She tried to deal with his infidelity and she just couldn't handle it at all. She didn't think the medication she was taking was helping her and at age 51 she took her own life, using prescription drugs.

MACK

Mack (age 52) was a construction worker, moved frequently, married three times, had four children, very close to his children, had a few periods of sobriety, refused all medication for his bipolar (manic depressive) condition, fought with people in A. A. over "rules" for A. A. (probably a species of irritable manic stages), resigned his service position in A. A., "went out" (started using drugs, then alcohol), after about a year put a shotgun in his mouth and pulled the trigger.

Now all of these people were popular and had friends, though in the end they couldn't see that they had friends. They were also attracted to partners who were highly intelligent. Now, why would these manic-depressive women be attracted to highly intelligent men (genius-type men)? Why would the men be attracted to highly intelligent women? Not sure I know the answer—but one of the possibilities is that the intelligence and the manic depression and the alcoholism are linked. My present husband (a clinical but not a manic depressive) is fond of quoting the poet's words, "Great wit is sure to madness near allied"—for whatever that's worth.

One thing is clear: the difference between manic depressive alcoholics who in one way or another take their life and those who don't is very much the difference between manic depressive alcoholics who don't take their medicine and those who do. A. A. alone doesn't do it. Dr. Carlos Zarate was right when he told me forty-five years ago, "A. A. for your alcoholism and lithium for your manic depression."

Kay Redfield Jamison's books deal with creativity and manic

depression (and another deals with suicide). On looking these brief biographies over, I am struck by the fact that all the deaths—and all the subjects—are in their 50s: I wonder if things are brought to a head by change-of-life conditions.

"Tricyclic antidepressants are aimed at norepinephrine balances, while amitryptaline (Elavil) aims at serotonin and acetylcholine, and the generation of selective serotonin re-uptake inhibitors (SSRIs, including Prozac) have their effect solely on serotonin. But what triggers the depression, of whatever type? The answer seems to be that cyclical manic depression (bipolarity) does not need an evident trigger, though it may have one. But even if there is a trigger, the subject 'may also carry an abnormal gene or two, which predispose to depression'" (p. 245).

Also, the "subjective experience of depression (of any kind) is the expression of the interplay between our brain regions that register and interpret our current emotional experiences in the light of our past emotional experiences" (ibid). Psychiatrists who are also neuroscientists are currently engaged in trying to see how the various distributed regions in the "extended limbic system" link together past memories, present experiences, and the attribution of "feeling tones" to these. It is this complicated set of interconnections that enables us to experience (subjectively) emotions such as sadness and (cognitively) attribute these figures to ourselves, as by saying, "Gee! I feel depressed today." Why women say this more often than men almost certainly has something to do with serotonin, but SSRIs do not work on manic depression, which is bipolar and for which the preferred treatment is the natural salt lithium...

It has been suggested that bipolar disorder may be related to the bipolarity of chaotic ordering, though it might be connected with lunar cycles and the tides. (A long-time member of A. A. has mentioned to me that when he came into the fellowship in the late 1940s there was a doctor who claimed that the tidal pull of the moon on brain fluids had something to do with periodic—Jellinek "epsilon"—drinking: the explanation need not be correct but the periodic pattern—the "periodicity"—might be—as with *luna*tics or *luna*cy generally.)

There are some indications that very rapidly cycling bipolarity might be a different condition (differently treatable) from the more common form. Now, bipolarity of either form is not unique to women, but it is heavily concentrated in women and highly creative men, particularly artists (schizophrenia seems more linked to highly creative mathematicians, as with John Nash). Unless we suggest that highly artistic men "have more of the woman in them" (which was indeed a commonplace from Tiresias to Leonardo), and considering the possibility of male menstrual cycles, it is not clear where this leaves us. But we know there are gender differences in alcoholics, and gender-concentrations in types of depression, so work on the biochemistry of manic depression may help us.

Let me quote here from the study that has had a significant effect on my thinking (Jared C. Lobdell, *This Strange Illness: Alcoholism and Bill W.* [Berlin: Aldine-DeGruyter 2004], p. 199). "After all, any cyclothymic disorder may reflect the influence of cyclic events on cortisol production [Andreasen, p. 236]. If ... alcoholics have lower than normal cortisol levels, it would mean that for self-preservation the alcoholic manic-depressive would need to be "up" more than her (or his) non-alcoholic counterpart—and we recall that one thing producing cortisol is stress. If we postulate an alcoholic (a young "born" alcoholic) who is a manic depressive with a first great depression ("triggered" perhaps by a parent's death ...), say at age twelve or thirteen, we might expect that she (more likely than he) would either start to drink (possibly in a periodic pattern at first), or at least engage in other stress-producing behavior, or both, to ameliorate the depressive phases of the condition (and, being young, enjoy the manic). Of course, the swings might be so violent even so that thoughts of suicide would still occur, but drinking and stress-seeking would be a prime example of self-medication for the bipolar disorder."

That's a description of me.

CONCLUSION

This has been the story of any "manic depressive"—any bipolar—
life, with a couple of Notes (on Treatment and on Relation to
Alcoholism), and then a chapter on how the relationship (to
alcoholism) and the bipolarity itself have affected my life at certain
junctures. I've taken definitions from common sources, including the
Mayo Clinic, and I've given a brief discussion of treatment as
commonly understood and prescribed. But I know from my own
experience, and from reading, particularly of recent discoveries (if
they are discoveries)—and I will continue to emphasize—that there's
what some might call a "spiritual" aspect to treatment or cure or
amelioration. I'm talking about physical—neuronal—changes that
seem at least in part physically inexplicable. Can prayer or dream or
vision or some other "cure within" really change the physical
configurations of the brain? I'm thinking maybe it really should be
something we're looking at. Partly, I suppose that may be from my
experience as an alcoholic—but a lot of the older data is already there
in the work of the founder of American clinical psychology, William
James—and he died more than a century ago.

As an alcoholic, I hope the principles I'm practicing in all my
affairs, in all my life, are love and service—this is my prayer as an
alcoholic. It's harder to put together a prayer for those afflicted with
a bipolar condition. But before we get to a prayer, I should say that in
my "up" periods, my pursuit of my A. A. ideals (including, in the
words of the Episcopal prayer, "a godly, righteous, and sober life") is
not always full speed ahead—I don't want it to be manic—and, more

important, in my "down" periods I have finally gotten it not to come to a full stop.

I can't quite use the same phrasing I used in the prayer at the end of my *Q & A: Alcoholism and Sobriety*. But it's close and just as heartfelt.

PRAYER

My prayer is that in reading this book you will find some of the
answers to this baffling disease of bipolar disorder or manic
depression. I hope you will find the answers I have found that will
make life somewhat easier for you. God bless you.

Love, Jane

Elizabethtown, Pennsylvania
October 2017

ABOUT THE AUTHOR

Jane S., originally from rural Pennsylvania, was first officially diagnosed as "Manic-Depressive" when she was thirty-one, after she was twenty-one months sober, but the symptoms had begun to appear when she had her first drink at fourteen. She was given "shock treatments" for her illness years before the official diagnosis. Now retired from the Pennsylvania Department of Corrections, she lives in Central Pennsylvania with her husband and her grandson, Jeffrey. Her son Andrew lives a few miles away in Lancaster. This is her second book, after *Q & A: Alcoholism and Sobriety* (Hindsfoot 2007). She has been sober since October 1970 and on successful Lithium therapy since July 1972.

More information can be found at: https://janesabc.wordpress.com/
.

www.ingramcontent.com/pod-product-compliance
Lightning Source LLC
Chambersburg PA
CBHW030253030426
42336CB00009B/365